If These **WALLS** *Could* **TALK:**
NEBRASKA CORNHUSKERS

Stories from the Nebraska Cornhuskers Sideline, Locker Room, and Press Box

Jerry Murtaugh with Jimmy Sheil, Brian Rosenthal,
George Achola, and Brian Brashaw

TRIUMPH
BOOKS

This book is available in quantity at special discounts for your group or organization. For further information, contact:

Triumph Books LLC
814 North Franklin Street
Chicago, Illinois 60610
(312) 337–0747
www.triumphbooks.com

Printed in U.S.A.

ISBN: 978-1-62937-153-5

Design by Amy Carter

CONTENTS

FOREWORD

It didn't take long to figure out that Nebraska football was different.

I was working in Monroe, Louisiana, in my last week as a sports reporter covering Louisiana Tech. With friends living in Nebraska, it made sense for me to follow the team to the opening game of the 1998 season in Lincoln. No one covering the Bulldogs thought they had a chance against the Huskers but it would be an opportunity to visit one of the cathedrals of college football.

The walk up to the game was different than any other scene I had witnessed at a college football game. I'd been to dozens of stadiums, from Happy Valley to Baton Rouge to the Rose Bowl, but this was different. It was the first time I had heard the "Go Big Red" chant. The first time I watched the Pride of Nebraska marching band travel through the crowd to its spot in the stadium. The first time I had a fan of an opposing team stop me to tell me how well they had been treated all morning at tailgates around town.

From Yankee Stadium to the Boston Garden, you have probably heard stories of the first time a fan walks out a tunnel to see the playing surface. My story isn't much different from those aside from the fact that I was working and trying to be professional. So many people in red, a buzz traveling through the sections about the start of a new season and era of Nebraska football, and the entire stadium singing the national anthem. It was a special experience for me but at the same time I could see in the eyes of the people around me that it was a special experience for long-time fans as well.

The biggest difference about Memorial Stadium and its fans for me, however, became clear after the game. Louisiana Tech receiver Troy Edwards had the single greatest day of catching a football in college history. Quarterback Tim Rattay had thrown the ball around, over and at times through the Blackshirt defense, but as I walked back in the tunnel area interviewing those guys, fans were cheering. The Rattay-Edwards combo had just had a record-setting day in their house, but the Husker fans couldn't stop complimenting the players from Ruston. It knocked me and the players back on our heels. Were people actually being this nice, saying these things and meaning them? It's a situation that I have seen many times over the last decade covering Nebraska football, but the memory of my first trip to the Old Gray Lady at 10th and Vine will always stick with me.

Like so many who have had the chance to walk through those gates.

—*Mike'l Severe*
Host of "The Bottom Line" on World-Herald Live

INTRODUCTION

I am the luckiest S.O.B. on the face of the earth thanks to everything that has happened in my life coming from north Omaha. People have helped me every step of the way, whether I deserved it or not. I owe that to playing football for the University of Nebraska.

As a high school senior at Omaha North, I was actually thinking of going to Oklahoma to play football and wrestle. The Sooners were offering me lots of nice things, but they got wind of it in Lincoln. Coach Bob Devaney came up to Omaha and talked me out of it.

I would not have played at Nebraska and had the life I did without Coach Devaney taking an extra interest in me, but we never saw eye to eye.

My playing days at Nebraska were a lot of fun and good for the program as we kept building on what Devaney started when he came from Wyoming in the early 1960s to be head coach. As many of the Husker fans know, my teams were pretty damn good and the fans know the team highlights from my time at Nebraska from 1967 to 1970.

But in this book, I want to share some of the stuff you guys don't know about—the interesting and funny stuff that happened in my career as a linebacker at Nebraska, the ups and downs, especially with Devaney.

What happened on the field was only part of the story of my time at Nebraska.

Jerry Murtaugh with his wife, Connie, on the night of their engagement in 2008. (He wasn't kidding about being lucky!) *(Courtesy of Jerry Murtaugh)*

From my freshman year not going to class to starting as a sophomore on varsity but having Oklahoma trounce us and a Heisman winner-to-be taunt me. To my junior year getting revenge on Oklahoma and then almost causing an international incident in Juarez, Mexico, on our bowl trip with teammates Bob "Fig" Newton and Wally Winter, among others. To my senior year getting kicked out of the Playboy Club in Chicago and later in the year kicking LSU's butt to win a national title. And then when Eddie Periard and I, celebrating after the game, went to the LSU hotel because we were drunk and somehow got in their rooms, because when you are drunk you can do almost anything you put your mind to.

But I not only want to share my stories—I want other Huskers to have the same chance. Doing a radio show in Omaha and Lincoln, I hear so many great stories that don't make the papers, and I know fans will enjoy them immensely. (I was going to say "enjoy them a lot," but my wife, Connie Ann, said I should try to use words that aren't so common. Even I can learn!)

So I think you guys will immensely enjoy reading the other Huskers stories too, including some from one of the first Blackshirts ever in Mike Kennedy from Omaha Benson. Also, we've put together many things even I didn't know before we wrote this book. Learn what Tom Osborne said on the sideline in 1978 before Jimmy Pillen pounced on a Sooner fumble to ice that epic win; read about a heart-to-heart talk between Osborne and Mitch Krenk when Osborne had to tell the young Krenk that the player had cancer; read about current Husker staff member and former player Kenny Wilhite getting shot before he came to Nebraska and how Osborne and Ron Brown responded.

We have some Heisman winners in Johnny Rodgers and Mike Rozier, and an All-American in Harry Grimminger, too. Also hear from other great Huskers like Barry Alvarez, Scott Raridon, Mike Anderson, Jay Foreman, Adam Carriker, Zac Taylor, John O'Leary, Matt Davison, and Jared Crick. And we didn't forget the most recent guys with stories from Mike Caputo and 2014 All-American Ameer Abdullah. Find out where Ameer was when Nebraska called him for the first time and why he almost didn't answer that fateful call late in the recruiting process.

Lastly, I'm not kidding that Devaney wanted to fistfight me. I would have....

Read on and enjoy!

—*Jerry Murtaugh*

CHAPTER 1

JERRY MURTAUGH, FRESHMAN YEAR

Linebacker, 1967

It's well known that Jerry Murtaugh was an All-American linebacker at Nebraska in 1970 and that he held the all-time NU tackles record until Barrett Ruud broke it in 2004. It is also somewhat well-known that Murtaugh greatly angered head coach Bob Devaney by predicting a National Championship before the 1970 season, and that Murtaugh was in Devaney's doghouse often, whether it was his mouth or laying out the quarterbacks in no-contact drills.

A few people know that Husker assistant coach John Melton had to pick up the pieces, so to speak, after "Murt" had a misstep (or felony) on the field, in the classroom, in the Lincoln streets, or in the bars. Melton was the good cop in some ways to Devaney's bad cop, and they weren't the only cops Murtaugh saw in his college career.

The Devaney and Murtaugh squabbles had been ongoing and heated since the Omaha North graduate's first semester on campus. In fact, in 2014 Murtaugh said on his weekly radio show that if he knew where Devaney's grave was he would go and...actually the story will stop there as Murt's comment elicited phone calls from angry, and shocked, listeners.

While the rocky relationship with Devaney is well-known, what isn't is how the trouble with Devaney started.

"How did I get on Bob's bad side? Hell, who knows? Oh wait...I know," Murtaugh said laughing. "I think I went to class three days out of the whole first semester my freshman year. I was thinking I'm a PE major so I don't have to go to class.

"That season I played freshman ball for the frosh coach Cletus Fischer and not much was said. I thought everything was okay."

That was until his first one-on-one meeting with Devaney at the end of the semester. An emergency meeting, no less.

"Devaney called me in when the semester was over and he told me I flunked nine out of 12 hours," Murtaugh said. "He told me I had two options—you flunk out or you go to class and get your grades up and go to summer school."

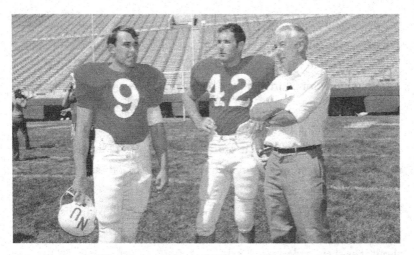

Jerry Murtaugh (42) with his dad and Erv Haynes (9) during the 1967 season. *(Courtesy of Jerry Murtaugh)*

Murtaugh would hardly become a Rhodes Scholar in the second semester, but he did straighten up for a little while.

"Second semester I went to school every day and I had like a C average," Murtaugh said. "My PE degree was in sight again."

While Murtaugh started going to class regularly during his second semester, trouble seemed to follow him around campus. But he was fortunate a teammate of his was usually at his side. A teammate who would be around for many of Murtaugh's off-the-field forays was Wally Winter, a 6'5" red-headed offensive lineman out of Eagle, Nebraska.

"My freshman year the night before the spring game, Wally and I decided to have a couple of drinks," Murtaugh said. "We go over to a fraternity house and we had a couple of beers. Then they had a street dance on campus so we decided to go check it out; I was not married yet."

A slow night turned fast quickly.

"So I go over there and I'm walking around minding my own business. Then I walk through a bunch of guys and all of sudden I got jumped," Murtaugh said. "I am getting beat up pretty good; there were at least four to five of them. Why they got me I don't know. I don't think I said anything to them…but I might have."

Thankfully for Murtaugh, the big lineman was not out on the dance floor.

"All I know is I'm on my back getting whupped and it is getting darker and darker and then it starts to get lighter and lighter as Waldo was pulling guys off me," Murtaugh said. "I'm all bloody and the cops are coming so we take off."

The two freshmen teammates made their way to the campus hospital with Murt needing attention and thinking his coaches would not hear about it as they made a quick exit.

"We go to the infirmary on campus to get stitched up. As I am getting worked on they hand me the phone. It's Devaney," Murtaugh said. "He heard some of what happened from the cops. And he was sorta yelling at me. He said 'What in the hell did you do this time?'

"And I'm just telling him that I didn't start this and I got jumped!"

Murtaugh got the medical attention he needed and the doctor sent him on his way. He thought the stitches were the end of it, but that was only a brief halftime in the fiasco.

"So I get home about 2:00 in the morning and I get another call from Devaney," Murtaugh said. "But this time he was screaming and yelling again and calling me names this time too. Devaney said, 'You son of a bitch Murtaugh! I heard what you did!'

"And again I said, 'I didn't do nuthin but get my ass kicked.'"

Murtaugh was not injured badly, with a swollen eye being the worst of it, but any ailment before an important game, like his first Spring Game at Nebraska, was concerning. The carefree Murtaugh was even concerned his eyesight would not be the same.

"Next day my eye is swollen shut and I look like a Cyclops and I could not see out of that eye at all," Murtaugh said. "So I get to the

Coach Bob Devaney during the 1967 season at Memorial Stadium. *(Courtesy of Jerry Murtaugh)*

stadium before anybody else and I got dressed and put my helmet on and just sat there.

"I did not want anyone to see my eye because I was scared. I didn't know how I was going to play. Thank god it was my bad eye though."

As would become a pattern in his college days, Melton would be there to try to sort things out and keep Murt on track.

"So I'm sitting there in the locker room and I get a knock on my helmet," Murtaugh said. "I go 'What?' and don't look around as I was pissed. And it was Coach Melton and he said, 'Murtaugh, what did you do?' "And I said I didn't do nothing."

Melton let him know the score with Devaney as Murtaugh's freshman year was wrapping up.

"Murtaugh, Devaney is madder than hell at you," Melton said, almost pleading with his linebacker to understand the situation. "Murtaugh, all I got to say is you better play good today!'"

However, Melton wanted to see the damage done, and initially Murt would not take off his helmet. Finally Murtaugh turned around and Melton's voice hit a new low (or high).

"OH MY GOD Murtaugh!" Melton exclaimed when he saw the one-eyed player. "Put your helmet back on...and you better play good today!'"

Fortunately for Murtaugh, the Cyclops linebacker would play well.

"I go out and I had a hell of a spring game. So that is how it all got started my freshman year," Murtaugh said. "And after that we just never got along. It would be a fight here, or I was thrown in jail there, or for a fight I was thrown in jail here, ya never knew what. Just stupid stuff.

Melton also had a long talk with Murtaugh about his decision-making and how it affected Melton's health.

"Poor ol' Melton told me, 'You are gonna kill me. You can't do this. Devaney is after me to control you,'" Murtaugh said.

"And finally he says, 'How can I control you, Murtaugh?'"

Murt had a typical response.

"You can't, coach. Just coach me," Murtaugh said, laughing.

"Yeah, it was probably my fault Bob and I got off to a bad start."

—*Jimmy Sheil*

CHAPTER 2

MIKE KENNEDY

Linebacker, 1962–65

As an undefeated Nebraska squad rolled toward a Big 8 title and a possible National Championship late in the 1965 season, the Huskers faced a decidedly inferior Oklahoma State team. The Cornhuskers coaches knew only one person, a "tough son of a gun," could ruin their trophy march that day and it was Oklahoma State Cowboys fullback and future Dallas Cowboys Pro Bowler, Walt Garrison.

The year before, Garrison was a relatively unknown player but Nebraska knew him well by the end of the game. He helped Oklahoma State keep it close late into the game by totaling 112 yards versus the Huskers on 26 touches in a game Nebraska won 27–14.

This Oklahoma State cowpoke was a real cowboy, as Garrison rode bulls for kicks during the summer and had been gauging Big 8 defenses all season on a team with no other weapons. So early in the week a Husker coach let one of the first-ever Blackshirts know he would get to know this bull rider well on game day.

In fact, Omaha Benson High School graduate Mike Kennedy probably could have skipped all team activities that week, and classes for that matter, as long as the linebacker showed up with bad intentions in Stillwater on Saturday afternoon for his lone assignment.

"Coach [George] Kelly pulled me aside early in the week," Kennedy said, "and told me to forget all my keys, reads, or whatever and just spy on that tough son of a gun, Walt Garrison, on every stinkin' play."

Heavily favored Nebraska did prevail at Oklahoma State 21–17 in 1965 to remain undefeated at 9–0, dropping Oklahoma State to 1–7 on the season, but not before Garrison and the Cowboys almost pulled the upset of the year to derail Nebraska's Orange Bowl and National Championship hopes.

Garrison had 19 carries for 121 yards, but Kennedy and company held him in check most of the day holding him to 77 yards on 17 carries until the final two plays. With the tension mounting on the game's final drive, Garrison ripped off a 26-yard run at midfield with less than a minute remaining.

And with just three seconds remaining, Oklahoma State had the ball on Nebraska's 23-yard line and everybody from Stillwater to Miami was thinking pass, where nervous Orange Bowl officials were thinking their planned announcement of Nebraska in the Orange Bowl would have to wait.

The Omaha World-Herald's iconic sportswriter Wally Provost described the last play—a run, not a pass—this way from the paper's famed November 13, 1965, Blue Streak Edition:

"Even as time ran out in this bloodcurdling drama, Walt Garrison broke loose on an 18-yard run to the N.U. five-yard line where valiant Huskers swarmed the defiant Cowpoke."

Kennedy was among those Huskers riding the bucking fullback until he dropped. The state of Nebraska heaved a sigh of relief, and the Cornhuskers clinched the Big 8 championship and an Orange Bowl berth. However, the redheaded Kennedy might not have been on the field that day in Oklahoma if he would have followed his military ambitions out of high school.

As a senior in high school in 1961, the Benson Bunny had a congressional appointment at the Air Force Academy and was weighing his college options. Also, Nebraska football wasn't the nationally renowned "Big Red" yet under then-Husker coach Bill Jennings, who coached at Nebraska from 1957 to 1961.

Enter new Husker coach Bob Devaney.

Upon being hired in January 1962, Devaney rounded up some film of players from the state of Nebraska. He saw Kennedy making plays and the coach made his way to Omaha. Kennedy was one of the first, if not the first, recruiting visits for the new coach. The folksy Devaney quickly demonstrated his people and recruiting skills by showing one of the Kennedy boys extra attention on his visit to the family's home.

Kennedy's older brother, Pat, was already a college football player at Fort Hayes State. However, at the start of the 1961 season, the Fort

Hayes sophomore felt winded quickly and had no energy. They ran some blood tests on Pat and sent him back to Omaha. Shortly thereafter, he was diagnosed with leukemia and began treatment for the deadly disease.

"Coach Devaney came to our house and I introduced him to all of my family," Kennedy said. "Then my brother, Pat, who was a real avid photographer, excused himself to go work on some photography in his darkroom in the basement.

"But then Coach Devaney asked my brother if he could go downstairs with him to look at his photography. And Devaney spent about 45 minutes with my brother in the basement, while me and my family sat upstairs looking at each other."

Finally, the coach reappeared and made his short recruiting pitch.

"Devaney came back upstairs and sat down with us for no more than five minutes," Kennedy said. "He just said to me, 'I want to offer you a full-ride scholarship to the University of Nebraska and if you want to come down, we would love to have you, Mike.'"

That short, but impactful, recruiting trip had an effect on Kennedy's dad, Dr. Paul Kennedy, a professor at the University of Nebraska at Omaha.

"After Devaney left, my dad looked at me and said, 'Ya know Mike, you might want to think about playing for that guy,'" Dr. Kennedy said.

Pat passed away a few months later from leukemia, just two days after Mike's high school graduation.

While Devaney brought him to Lincoln, another coach—who would be a head coach at Nebraska someday, too—had an unusual initial encounter with Kennedy brought on by a mutual interest. A graduate assistant coach at the time, Tom Osborne, had heard the middle linebacker was known to go fishing often, so one day Osborne asked if he might be able to go with him.

The outgoing Kennedy was only too glad to oblige his fellow redhead. They spent many afternoons around the state of Nebraska at ponds and

Mike Kennedy having a well-earned orange slice after a win at home in 1965.
(Courtesy of Mike Kennedy)

lakes where more fishing than talking was usually done. However, another time, Osborne showed he wasn't always so reserved.

At the time Nebraska had a quality, and boisterous, defensive back in Ted Vactor from Washington, D.C. Vactor was eventually an All-Big 8 selection and one day would play for the Washington Redskins and Chicago Bears in the pros.

Aside from returning punts, Vactor was good at letting people know how fast he was. Maybe Cassius Clay (who would later become known as Muhammad Ali) inspired Vactor to have some good-natured fun with his mouth and abilities. But one day, Osborne, a former college star and NFL player, had heard enough.

"One time toward the end of practice Ted was blowing smoke about how fast he was and nobody could beat him," Kennedy said. "And finally

Tom had heard enough and said to Vactor, 'Let's make a deal. We race and if you win, you don't do 40s at the end of practice and I run in your place. I win and you are the only one that runs.'

"Of course Ted was cocky as ever and he took the bet. And ya know what? Vactor got smoked by Tom with those long strides."

Kennedy reminded Osborne of this bet recently.

"So right when Tom came back to Nebraska as the athletic director in 2007, I sent him a note saying, 'I know we are in good hands because anybody that could shut Vactor up, can handle anything.'"

As is Osborne's nature, he replied to Kennedy with a lighthearted note of thanks.

Kennedy's Nebraska career began on the freshman team in the fall of 1962, and he found it uneventful, mostly due to only having only two games on the freshman schedule. However, the future All-Big 8 linebacker did start his Nebraska career as a halfback and returned punts as well. From newspaper reports at the time, Kennedy was called "speedy" and weighed about 190 at 5'11".

But it was during this time of nonstop freshman practices and occasional practices with the varsity that any of his doubts about playing in college football were erased. He realized he belonged at this level, as he did not feel overwhelmed by the varsity players, and set a goal of starting by his junior year.

His varsity Husker career would start in the spring of 1963 with spring practice. One Nebraska staff member who took note of Kennedy's talent was running backs coach Mike Corgan, since Kennedy was still a halfback. However, Kennedy would have remembered the demanding Corgan regardless of position for his old-school approach, even for the 1960s.

It might have been out of character for Osborne to challenge a player, even in good fun with Vactor, but that was standard operating procedure for Corgan. Just as common as his corncob pipe, Corgan did not hesitate to push or confront a player to be successful, or if need be, to push him out of the country.

On Nebraska's roster at the time was a Canadian running back/receiver that could run, or "fly" as Kennedy put it, but he was "allergic" to contact. This allergy did not bode well for a player under Corgan. This player went by the moniker of "Canadian Jeff."

At the time, Nebraska ran a drill called Backs on Ends, in which basically two running backs would meet two linebackers in the hole and butt heads. The players would say about this drill, "Corgan ain't gonna be happy until he sees blood!"

One day that spring they were running the drill with its usual ferocity but with an extra-large group. Maybe sensing a bigger group could make him less noticeable and it might be his blood that day, Canadian Jeff, was able to get to the front of the drill line but get to the back of the line without ever taking his turn.

The plan was working fine until Corgan noticed the Canadian was not giving or taking any lumps.

"Corgan starts screaming when he sees Jeff is not taking his turn," Kennedy said. "He yells for him to get to the front of the line. He made him go seven or eight times in a row. And ol' Jeff got the snot beat out of him, but he finished practice."

That night Canadian Jeff left the country. When told of the departure, Corgan said he would be better off in Canada anyway. Corgan was right, as Jeff Atcheson played in the CFL for seven years and was a good kick returner in the more wide-open style of Canadian professional football.

Another pair of Huskers assistant coaches who worked together closely were defensive coaches Jim Ross and John Melton, who had an interesting dynamic according to Kennedy.

"Jim Ross, our secondary coach, he was a smart one!" Kennedy said. "When it came to football, he said less but knew more than anyone. And John Melton, our linebackers coach, was the coach who said more but knew less than anyone."

Translation: the good-natured Melton was usually the front man on recruiting and Ross was more into the Xs and Os of football. Also, Ross was the coach Devaney often came to for counsel and his opinions more than the other coaches. Ross had been with Devaney since their high school teaching and coaching days in the 1940s in Alpena, Michigan.

Devaney made a position change for Kennedy to start the 1963 season. While he had been a standout halfback as a freshman, they moved him to guard. The head coach told Hal Brown of the *Star Sports* paper in Lincoln that the move was a natural as Kennedy "likes to hit."

The position switch made him come directly into contact with a future college football and professional football Hall of Famer in Bob Brown. Kennedy was a sophomore when Brown was a senior and would occasionally face him in practice.

And courtesy of the one–platoon system, where players had to go both ways, there were some interesting practices with Brown as a linebacker and Kennedy as an offensive guard. Kennedy noted Brown had a way of dropping offensive lineman in the Big 8, but he was determined not to fall victim.

"Brownie had a move he called the Hammer. He was so big and so strong that he would let the offensive guard come into his body and block him," Kennedy said. "But when they got into him, Brownie then would come down with his arm right in the small of the blocker's back and immediately the blocker went down with the wind knocked out of him. I saw him do it all the time."

The first time Kennedy went against Brown live in a practice, he had a plan. He was going to be different than the many felled Big 8 blockers and not take the bait.

"In practice versus Brownie I told myself, 'I ain't gonna get the Hammer. I ain't gettin' the Hammer," Kennedy said. "So I went low and I cut him by blocking him low and it worked okay. And you better believe I scrambled away quickly.

Mike Kennedy with fellow captain Frank Solich (right) at a fundraiser before the Orange Bowl versus Alabama in 1966. *(Courtesy of Mike Kennedy)*

"After practice he came up to me and said, 'You did a good job out there today...but you ain't gonna be cutting me low like that again.'"

Kennedy nodded his understanding and knew Brown would not be so easy in the future, but practicing against Brown helped him develop as a player in 1963, even if he was not a starter yet for the Huskers.

Kennedy was one of the first players off the bench and was a regular contributor on both sides of the ball. Devaney's first Big 8 Championship came in 1963, and the regular season was capped off with a memorable win over Oklahoma just a day after President John F. Kennedy's assassination.

Mike Kennedy remembers preparing for the Oklahoma game that they might not play being a surreal experience. After a call from Robert Kennedy, they went ahead with the game and Nebraska went on to a 29–20 win over Oklahoma and earned a spot in the Orange Bowl, where they defeated Auburn and ended the season ranked fifth in the national polls.

At the end of 1963 it looked like Kennedy would be ready to take on a bigger role the following season, but an offseason rule change would alter the depth chart considerably.

Prior to 1964, college football players played both ways because of limited substitution rules. It was done for budget reasons, and a team could not change more than one player at a time. For the 1964 season, the NCAA changed the sub rule to be unlimited, which allowed teams to have specialized offensive and defensive players. Kennedy was all for it.

"I was the happiest guy in the world when the coaches told us the NCAA changed the rule on substitutions," Kennedy said. "[Defensive line coach George] Kelley said we are now one-way players and we could forget everything we ever learned about offense. I was elated.

"But Corgan hated to lose me because I never cared about carrying the ball; I just liked hitting people."

That rule change inadvertently started one of the most storied traditions in not only Nebraska football history, but all of college football. The Blackshirt tradition started simply enough, with a coach telling the starters to grab a certain color out of a bag full of jerseys. They called out the starters and said to get a black scrimmage vest out of a bag, Kennedy said.

Kennedy was only a linebacker and a first-time starter in 1964 as a junior. He led the team in tackles with 76 and his freshman feeling of belonging was validated. It was that season the term "Black Shirt" first appeared in the media and eventually changed to just one word, Blackshirts. For that season, Nebraska's defense was ranked second in the country. Other defensive stalwarts on that team were Vactor and middle guard Walt Barnes.

Vactor and Barnes were on a starting defense for which Kennedy called the plays on Saturday afternoons. Kennedy had this assignment because of his off-the-field work ethic according to a Husker defensive assistant coach.

"I think he has diagnostic abilities," Coach Kelly said in Curt Mosher's column in the *Lincoln Journal* during the 1964 season. "He has called in the past a real fine defensive game because he devotes a good deal of his time to watching film each week to establish tendencies of the opposing team. And he's a fine leader and he likes to hit people." Hitting people and dropping them was one of the reasons Kennedy was seen as a leader going into the 1965 season. His status as a leader was validated on the team when he was elected as a captain, along with feisty fullback Frank Solich, at the start of the season.

One time the captains had an unusual coin toss with some Missouri players Kennedy had come to know through their battles on the field: Tiger captains Johnny Roland and Bruce Van Dyke. When they went out for the coin flip that day in Columbia, Missouri, at Faurot Field, Van Dyke looked a little quizzical at the smaller Solich, but Kennedy quickly let him know he best be ready for Nebraska's bruising fullback.

"Bruce, don't get fooled by his size. He will knock your ass into the dirt," Kennedy said to the Missouri player. "Then Frank got mad at me and told me to shut up, then all of us, including the ref, started laughing, but ol' Frank kept his game face on."

While Devaney had the two-time champs poised for a third straight Big 8 title, their practice routine for 1965 was changed up a bit. They began to scrimmage ones versus ones more often and this had painful consequences for one Huskers offensive player. Kennedy said the newly christened Blackshirts were ready for this as team bragging rights were on the line. On this particular August day, the defense was having their way with the offense.

"We were fired up and we were just annihilating the offense," Kennedy said. "Every running play they would lose yards, and every pass play we would intercept the ball or knock the crap out of somebody."

Frustrations soon set in for the offense on the lightly officiated scrimmage and some offensive players were holding just to survive. This was greatly upsetting one defensive lineman, Langston "Trey" Coleman.

By this point in his Huskers career, Coleman had shown he was a young man of strong will and toughness. More than that, he was without a doubt the last guy you wanted to make mad on a team with its share of knuckleheads.

Coleman grew up in a rough section of Washington, D.C. His mother worked for a native of the Cornhusker state, Ted Sorensen, who was an adviser to President Kennedy. Coleman mowed Sorensen's lawn growing up so he got to know about the midwestern state and its football team early on and it caught his interest.

Coleman basically hitchhiked as a walk-on from Washington, D.C. to Lincoln and earned a scholarship. He had a way of resolving the obstacles in front of him, and the flagrant holding in practice would be no different.

"In the scrimmage a player is holding Langston constantly and Langston is yelling at the coaches that this guy is holding, but nobody would do anything," Kennedy said. "In the huddle we were telling him to relax as we were killing them, but he was just fuming and it kept happening."

Finally Coleman calmed down but it was only after he said to the guy holding him, "I will take care of you later."

Kennedy knew this meant it would be handled in his way and he thought to himself, *Oh no! This ain't good.*

Practice ended with no more flare-ups and the players went into the locker room and some figured the trouble Coleman and the teammate had was over. After practice in those days there would be orange slices and 7-Up bottles for refreshment in the locker room.

"I'm changing and drinking my bottle of pop in the locker room," Kennedy said. "Then out of the corner of my eye, I see Trey hit the other player over the head with a 7-Up bottle. BAM! And just lays him out cold."

Chaos and a circle quickly formed around the knocked-out player with trainer George Sullivan going to work while throwing his hands up in the air. Finally Devaney broke through the crowd and instinctively screamed at Coleman and asked what happened.

Mike Kennedy's brother, Pat, in the early 1960s shortly before being diagnosed with leukemia, which would eventually take his life in 1962. *(Courtesy of Fort Hayes University)*

Langston just looked at Devaney and replied matter-of-factly, "I told the guy to quit holding me."

In that situation, Kennedy showed he had some common sense, even though he was not successful in calming down his teammate. This even-keeled nature made Kennedy a good fit to be captain but also for another special job. Kennedy had a part-time role as he drove Devaney to and from golf outings and fundraisers around the state of Nebraska.

In some ways the younger Kennedy was Devaney's guardian at the events to keep him on schedule. A trip to the York Country Club in the summer before Kennedy's senior year was especially memorable after a round of golf and a fundraising dinner.

"On our way to York I asked, 'What time did you tell Phyllis you would be home?' and [Coach Devaney] said, 'Midnight,'" Kennedy said. "After golf we went our own way. After dinner it was getting late, so I went to get him.

"And of course he wanted to stay longer, but I said 'I'm not having you home late and facing Phyllis!' I just grabbed him and we headed out."

They got into the car and began the trip back to Lincoln. Kennedy asked the coach how the University of Nebraska did, so to speak.

"Devaney said 'I dunno, we got some checks.' And he then proceeded to pull out all these checks from everywhere. I mean everywhere!" Kennedy said. "Pants pockets, coats pockets, and shirt pockets stuffed with checks. Some are falling all over the front seat."

Kennedy took the checks from Devaney to organize them and then put them in his own pockets. However, Kennedy forgot to give the checks back when he dropped off Devaney. The coach was tired from a long fundraising day, and he was content to get out of the car and to the front door, oblivious to the fact that he didn't have the checks.

But first thing in the morning, it was the only thing on Devaney's mind. He made a panicked phone call at 8:00 AM and asked Kennedy if he had the checks.

"I knew I had them but I said, 'What? Now why would I have them?'" Kennedy said. "But finally the panic was too much and I told coach I had them. He then called me EVERY name in the book and some I have never heard before."

There were also some good comments from Devaney mixed in later in the 1965 season as Kennedy led the team in tackles for the second straight season, with 69. However, leading the team in tackles came with a price for Kennedy as the injuries began to pile up, but he was usually at his linebacking spot according to his head coach at the end of the season in an *Omaha World-Herald* column by Wally Provost.

"When the band starts to play," Devaney said, "they put a little tape on Mike and he's out there."

After a taped-up Kennedy and Nebraska subdued Oklahoma State and Garrison late in the 1965 season, the Huskers made quick work of Oklahoma to finish the regular season undefeated. The Big 8 champs were also ranked number three in the country. The Huskers' 10–0 record set up an Orange Bowl game between undefeated Nebraska and No. 4–ranked Alabama.

As was becoming customary at the time, bowl games were more than just a football game, with more pageantry. The local and national media began to cover the game from a human-interest angle. Kennedy's family would get in on the act courtesy of the *Lincoln Star* newspaper.

For their coverage of the Orange Bowl that season, the Lincoln paper had a "special correspondent." Giving Huskers fans a unique look at the game through a daily diary would be Kennedy's wife, Lucy, in a column called "Orange Bowl Chatter." The two had been high school sweethearts and married in 1963. This would be her third bowl game overall and second Orange Bowl as the paper referred to her in the byline as "Lucy (Mrs. Mike) Kennedy."

In her first installment, Lucy reported back to Nebraskans that her flight to Miami was mostly wives of players and staff along with NU administration. The team and coaches took another flight. She observed NU athletic director Tippy Dye, team physician Dr. Paul, and NU sports information director Don Bryant playing cards.

Maybe Lucy could not print how much everybody's favorite Sports Information Director lost?

"Don Bryant concluded that by the end of the afternoon he was not very good at cards," Lucy Kennedy wrote.

Later in the week, she noted a fad in swimwear was taking hold around their hotel: the bikini. She also succinctly described the preparation of the players, coaches, and fans for the big game in and around the team's hotel, the famous Ivanhoe.

"Boating, swimming, fishing, sightseeing trips, shopping and, we understand, a bit of golf is helping to build the Cornhusker's endurance for the Orange Bowl game—and then there are other slothful fans doing nothing but tanning and eating," Lucy penned back to Nebraska in the dead of winter.

Lucy was reporting on a big bowl game (with its slothful fans), but it became a bigger game thanks to the results from some other bowl games early on New Year's Day. The two teams ranked ahead of Nebraska and Alabama in the polls both lost. This meant the Husker–Crimson Tide Orange Bowl game would be for the National Championship.

Unfortunately for Nebraska, Bear Bryant's team raced to a 24–7 halftime lead and ended up winning 39–28. According to Kennedy, the game wasn't as close as the final score. Devaney's first National Championship would have to wait, but there was no waiting for Kennedy to start the next phase of his life —his playing days were over. He did look into playing professional football but it was a quick look.

The Green Bay Packers offered him a $1,000 signing bonus and $4,500 if he made the team. Kennedy declined because he would make more as a teacher. He did his student-teaching to complete his education degree in the summer and graduated in August 1966.

While Kennedy did not have a pro career, Nebraska did not forget one of the first Blackshirts and stars of the Devaney era. In the late 1990s, Kennedy was elected to the Nebraska Football Hall of Fame. He took the field at Memorial Stadium one last time at halftime of the UAB game in 1998 with other inductees. But this time there was no No. 69 on his chest; Kennedy was clad in a red shirt, cowboy boots, jeans, and a handlebar mustache.

After his days as a Blackshirt, Kennedy used his education degree to become a high school teacher and coach, just like a young Devaney. Kennedy coached at various Omaha Public Schools before retiring in the 1990s, including his alma mater Omaha Benson. He also had a passion before its time in the 1960s and 1970s—competitive weightlifting. Kennedy traveled the country, winning many competitions with bests of a 700-pound squat, a 435-pound bench press, and a 665-pound dead-lift.

However, how exciting can a 700-pound squat be when you had to dance with that bull-rider Walt Garrison on every stinkin' play for an afternoon?

—Jimmy Sheil

CHAPTER 3

BARRY ALVAREZ

Linebacker, 1964–67

Barry Alvarez would lead the Huskers in tackles in 1967 among linebackers, but he was a nuisance all week long for offenses.

"Barry was the toughest player I ever had to block in a game or a practice," said Huskers teammate and tight end Dennis Morrison. "I just couldn't move him. Barry was just a physical, tough kid from Pennsylvania."

The tough kid from the east coast wanted to play in a bowl game as he was looking over colleges while attending Union High School in Burgettstown, Pennsylvania. He had many offers from teams playing on New Year's Day, including Nebraska, which was matched up with Auburn in the Orange Bowl following the 1963 season.

However, Nebraska had an in with Alvarez.

University of Nebraska assistant coach John Melton went to the same high school as Alvarez, and Melton recruited in the Pennsylvania area where Alvarez lived. Melton convinced Alvarez to make a trip to Lincoln, Nebraska, and see the campus of the rising power in the Big 8 Conference. Alvarez knew when he got there that football was important—to the school, to the state, and to the fans.

On the recruiting trip Alvarez admits to being impressed with everything: the players, Coach Devaney, and a team that finally broke Oklahoma's winning streak. But it was Melton who sealed the deal for Alvarez. Melton would also give Alvarez a hard time about his speed throughout his Husker career since his calling card was hitting people in the mouth.

Alvarez told Huskers.com that Melton used to tell him and another plodding linebacker, "If you two ever got in a footrace, neither one of you would win."

Alvarez played on the freshman team in 1964 and began to learn the ropes. That year Nebraska played in the Cotton Bowl against No. 10 Arkansas. The Huskers faced off against the Razorbacks but lost their bid for glory 10–7.

Alvarez knew he found a home with the University of Nebraska his sophomore year when he didn't want to return home for the summer, staying with friends in Lincoln.

Over Thanksgiving break, Alvarez bought a car for $50 and took off on a road trip with his teammate Mick Ziegler and a girlfriend. The trio stopped in Scottsbluff, Nebraska, to change the oil and forgot to put the oil cap back on.

As will happen without an oil cap, the engine melted but they managed to limp the car to a gas station in Lexington, Nebraska. A rancher named Norm Reynolds saw the crew and asked where they were from.

Upon learning the guys were Nebraska football players, Norm asked Alvarez which bowl game they were going to this year and then handed them the keys to his car with instructions to leave the keys under the mat when they returned.

Alvarez and Reynolds would remain friends, and the relationship would later shape Alvarez's post-playing career decision to start his coaching career in Lexington. It's fitting that one fateful event—meeting a Lexington rancher who showed him kindness—would set the tone for another one of Alvarez's life lessons forged in Lexington: connecting with the community. After his days in Lexington, Alvarez knew how to formulate relationships and build loyalty.

In 1965 the Huskers went 10–0 and won the Big 8 championship. They earned a trip to the Orange Bowl where they faced off against No. 4 Alabama.

At the half, the Crimson Tide held a 24–7 lead. The Huskers narrowed the lead to 24–13 with a 49-yard touchdown pass, but the momentum was with the Tide. The Huskers lost their Bowl bid 39 –28. But Alvarez got a taste of big-time football as a backup.

In 1966 the Huskers went 9–2 and would get a rematch with Alabama. But the Crimson Tide rolled to 34–7 in the Sugar Bowl. Of note for the season: Alvarez had two interceptions while seeing the field as a part-time starter.

In 1967, Alvarez led Nebraska in tackles among linebackers and helped the defense set a record of 40 forced turnovers. Alvarez and teammates like halfback Ben Gregory and mid-guard Wayne Meylan were seemingly bowl bound but some close losses kept them out of the picture.

Alvarez recalls Meylan as a tough farm kid. The guys would jump him and Meylan would throw them with zero effort like a man tossing little kids. Gregory, nicknamed The Pope, played both sides of the ball. He was a physical and very athletic player.

Alvarez recalls playing against a tough Missouri team that year, when a large offensive tackle named Russell Washington blindsided him three times. He said to Husker defensive back, Harry Meagher "Keep that SOB off of me!" Harry replied, "Fuck you! Fend for yourself! I am trying to survive!"

Alvarez attributes the Nebraska team success in the 1960s to the coaching staff assembled by Devaney. He said the coaches challenged the players and took them from good players to great players. Assistant coach Tom Osborne would become a wildly successful head coach for 25 years at Nebraska. Coach Devaney would be recognized as a trend-setter with innovative ideas and team building. Strength coaching, out-of-season conditioning, and walk-on principles were all implemented by Devaney—ideas which Alvarez later employed in his coaching career.

In an interview with ESPN, Alvarez said, "A lot of my philosophy was based upon the foundation I had starting at Nebraska."

Alvarez said the coaches had values, an amazing work ethic, and were friendly and open. Alvarez and John Melton remained friends and ended up working together later in Alvarez's career.

Almost immediately as head coach at Wisconsin, Alvarez implemented a walk-on program. Like Nebraska's program, this encouraged players who loved the team to play, especially those motivated without the need for scholarships. Alvarez also implemented, according to ESPN, Nebraska's notorious run game and impenetrable defense. The seeds of success were planted not only in Alvarez the Cornhuskers linebacker but also in Alvarez the winning coach.

While in graduate school, Alvarez became a graduate assistant coach for Nebraska and it seemed he was destined to follow in his famous coaches' paths, but he also worked as a police officer. Joe Carroll, an ex-player, was the captain of the Lincoln police department who hired football players in the summers. Alvarez started as a beat cop and worked his way up to detective. He was offered entry into the FBI, but his life was destined for another path.

Alvarez started as an assistant coach at Lincoln Northeast High School, where he spent three years. Working with new head coach Bob Els, they both grew as coaches and took the team to the state championship. Alvarez's hard work was rewarded when he was offered the head coaching position at Lexington High School in Lexington, Nebraska, where he coached for two years. Then, the superintendent of the high school in Mason City, Iowa, called Alvarez, stating that he had conducted two sets of interviews for a head coach and had been unsuccessful. Barry had no interest. The superintendent suggested Alvarez bring his wife up for the weekend, and his wife thought they should check it out. Having a clear schedule, they made the trip.

Mason City was in serious need of complete restructuring and Alvarez ended up taking the job. The next year, under Alverez's tutelage, Mason City became state champions. This got the attention of Iowa coach, Hayden Fry, and Notre Dame's Lou Holtz, both of whom, in addition to Bob Devaney, became Alvarez's biggest influencers. Coach Fry from the University of Iowa needed a recruiter from the state high schools and Alvarez created an effective network of high school coaches to add depth and talent to the Iowa bench. The Iowa Hawkeyes went to six bowl games in the eight years Alvarez lent his coaching skills.

Holtz of Notre Dame hired Alvarez initially as a linebackers coach and took him on as an assistant coach and then defensive coordinator in 1988. In the three seasons Alvarez was coaching in South Bend, the Irish went 32–5 and won the 1988 National Title. While Fry and Holtz had different philosophies, Alvarez acknowledged that both coaches could reach the same end result, which lent to Alvarez's coaching arsenal and eventually enhanced his success.

Alvarez's coaching career went full stride when he became the head coach for the University of Wisconsin, becoming the winningest coach in school history. This was no easy feat as Wisconsin had not had much success. Upon his arrival, 52 guys quit. Alvarez said he didn't miss them. Alvarez recalls that the facilities were inadequate at best, the team had only been to six bowl games ever, and they had not had a good team since 1962.

Alvarez knew what he had to do—start from scratch. He recruited top talent, improved facilities, and won over local high school coaches. His first win was a Big Ten title in 1993 and a Rose Bowl win under UCLA. The Wisconsin Badgers, under Alvarez as head coach, racked up a 119–74–4 record. Barry led the team to three Big Ten titles and three Rose Bowl appearances.

In 2005, Alvarez stepped down as the coach at Wisconsin and became the Athletics Director, a position he still holds. His list of achievements, according to UWBadgers.com, includes:

- Named head coach of Wisconsin days after his 42nd birthday—a grand personal achievement
- Became winningest coach in school history
- Coached three Big Ten and Rose Bowl Championships
- 10th coach in Big Ten history with 100 victories at a conference institution
- Coached five national award winners
- Guided Wisconsin to back-to-back Big Ten titles in 1998 and '99
- Coached four of the five winningest team in school history
- Named AFCA Coach of the Year in 1993
- Named Big Ten Coach of the Year in 1993 and 1998

- Awarded the Victor's Award 1999 National Coach of the Year
- Earned the 2004 AFCA Region 3 Coach of the Year
- Inducted into the Pennsylvania, Washington County Hall of Fame in 2000
- Received the Distinguished Alumnus Award from the University of Nebraska Lincoln in 2003
- Finalist for ESPN's Coach of the Decade in 1999
- Named to the 100 Most Influential Hispanics list in October 2001
- Cindy and Barry Alvarez co-campaign for Gilda's Club, a free support center for families dealing with cancer

Alvarez became the Athletic Director at the University of Wisconsin for the 2004–05 season. He came out of retirement from coaching in 2004–05 to wear the head coach position as well as athletic director. He proved his coaching credentials once again, leading the team to a 10–3 season and a trip to the Capital One Bowl where the Badgers upset No. 7–ranked Auburn 24–10. He also guided the Badgers in the 2013 Rose Bowl against Stanford. The Badgers lost 20–14 in a heavy–hitting slugfest.

Alvarez says the AD job keeps him busy but so does his eight grand-kids. In his free time, Alvarez travels with his wife. He has a home in Naples, Florida, and family in Spain. But he still keeps an eye on Nebraska; they are a Big Ten foe and the Nebraska athletic director worked for him at Wisconsin.

Of current Nebraska AD, Shawn Eichorst, Alvarez said, "He is a really smart guy. Nebraska is in good hands!"

While he used to challenge him on the field, Morrison said Alvarez's off-the-field work has been just as impressive.

"What Barry did at Wisconsin coaching and building the football team was phenomenal," Morrison said. "The whole athletic program at Wisconsin is one of the top tier programs in college sports."

—George Achola

CHAPTER 4

BOB NEWTON

Offensive Tackle, 1969–70

A native of La Mirada, California, Bob Newton grew up wanting to play where most college football hopefuls living in southern California dreamed of playing in the 1960s—the University of Southern California.

Newton's idol was a player by the name of Ron Yary, a two-time All-American for USC who became a Hall of Fame player for the Minnesota Vikings. A 6'5", 255-pound tackle, Yary played 15 seasons in the NFL and was named All-Pro for six straight seasons.

"I knew his brother really well, and Ron was like three or four years older than me, and Ron went to Cerritos College, and I was going to Cerritos College," Newton said, referring to the junior college in California, "so I kind of wanted to follow in Ron Yary's footsteps."

Newton also played offensive tackle and had a frame similar to that of Yary. Newton stood 6'4" and weighed 248 pounds. After his sophomore year at Cerritos, Newton felt his dream would soon become reality. He, too, would be a Trojan.

"USC called me and they said, 'We're interested in you, Bob. We're going to get back to you and we think you can be a USC Trojan,'" Newton said.

At the same time, Newton was being recruited by Barry Switzer, an assistant coach at the time for Oklahoma, and by Terry Donahue, the future UCLA coach who was an assistant coach at Kansas under Pepper Rodgers at that time.

Nebraska also showed interest. The Cornhuskers were coming off a disappointing 6–4 season in 1967—soon to be followed by another 6–4 season in 1968—and had been beaten by Alabama in bowl games following the 1965 and 1966 seasons by what coach Bob Devaney felt were smaller, quicker, faster offensive linemen. Devaney wanted to follow that model but wasn't having positive results.

His assistant coach and offensive coordinator, Tom Osborne, suggested pursuing junior college players. They'd be experienced, have two years to play and could help accelerate the model's development. Osborne also suggested searching talent-laden southern California in the process.

"[Nebraska] had not recruited out of California on a regular basis, so it was quite a challenge for Coach Osborne to get me interested in Nebraska," Newton said. "When he came and recruited me, he came to my house and he told me, 'Bob, we're going to be playing Oklahoma this weekend on national TV'—this is 1968—and he said, 'I want you to watch us and see what you think.'"

Newton awoke Saturday morning eager to watch the game. He turned on the TV and watched as Nebraska got blown out by Oklahoma 47–0. "The first thing that came to my mind was, 'Yeah, they need some help, all right,'" Newton said.

So Newton agreed to visit Lincoln on what would be his first recruiting visit. He'd never been out of southern California, and he flew to Nebraska in late December. Newton was on his visit alongside another recruit, Bob Terrio, a fullback from Fullerton, California.

"I got off the plane and I think it was like two or three degrees there in Lincoln," Newton said. "I had this kind of a thin mustache, and after about 10 yards walking from the plane, it was frozen. That's before they had the tarmac, and you had to walk to the inside of the building, so it was a pretty significant walk.

"Before I even got to the building, I said, 'There ain't no way I'm coming to the University of Nebraska. Too cold.' Coach Osborne and coach Jim Ross met us there in the building to pick us up. Coach Osborne, I remember he said later, the way I looked, he thought it wasn't really going to happen, that neither one of us was going to come back to Nebraska just because of the cold."

Newton not only disliked the weather, but he'd already heard from USC. Essentially he was telling the likes of Oklahoma and Kansas and Nebraska he'd be going to Los Angeles to play football. It was only a matter of time.

Too much time, as it turned out.

As the national letter of intent signing day inched closer, Newton still hadn't heard back from USC like the school had promised.

"So I called them, 'Hey, this is Bob Newton here at Cerritos College. You said you'd call me a month or two ago and said you were going to recruit me, and I haven't heard back from you, and I'd like to know what's going on,'" Newton said.

"They said, 'Who's this again?' First of all, they put me on hold, 'Hang on a second, Bob.' They came back two minutes later, 'We found some problems with your transcripts and we can't get you in.'"

Newton was certain his transcripts weren't an issue, but he received the message, loud and clear: USC didn't want him, had no intention of taking him, and maybe never did.

Newton told the school he understood, hung up the phone, and immediately called Osborne. He told him he was coming to Nebraska.

"Coach Osborne, he's the one who personally recruited me," Newton said. "He spent a lot of time recruiting me, a lot of phone calls, visited me. He had a major impact on me my whole life, as far as education. I ended up going back to school to get my bachelor's degree and my master's degree. He put a high emphasis on education."

But how and why did Newton so quickly choose the Cornhuskers after getting snubbed by USC?

Easy. He'd seen Nebraska's 1969 and 1970 football schedules.

USC was on both of them.

"Resentment and anger [are] good for football," Newton said.

Nebraska opened at home with USC in 1969, but Newton, just beginning his first season as a transfer, wouldn't crack the starting lineup until the Cornhuskers' fourth game, at Missouri. He played only the fourth quarter against the No. 5 Trojans, and although unranked Nebraska lost 31–21, Newton was excited to simply see the field.

His senior season was a different story. The USC game was played at

Bob Newton (74) in 1970 with teammates Jerry Tagge (14), Jeff Kinney (35), Guy Ingles (88), Van Brownson (12) and coach Bob Devaney. *(Courtesy of Bob Newton)*

the storied Los Angeles Coliseum. The Trojans were ranked No. 3 and Nebraska No. 9. Close to 75,000 fans attended. Nebraska forged ahead a couple of times only to have USC answer in a back-and-forth slugfest. The offensive line was setting the tone, and Newton battled against a player named Tody Smith, a 6'5", 250-pound defensive end from Beaumont, Texas.

"Joe Orduna, who was our running back, had a 67-yard run that game," Newton said. "John McKay, who was the head coach at USC at that time, said it was one of the best runs he'd ever seen and compared it to O.J. Simpson's runs."

This was also the first season that Osborne had installed the I-formation at Nebraska, and Newton, knowing Osborne was the brains behind the offense, always felt the team was in good hands with Osborne as offensive coordinator.

"Joe had cut to the right, then he cut back to the left and took it all the way for a touchdown. On that play, I had a pull to the right and cut Tody Smith down. I pulled and I cut him down just enough to where Joe Orduna ran right by him, and Tody was on the ground and kind of stretched out his arm, and he was about a foot short of reaching him. The timing of the block was well-executed, and the run was very well executed by Joe."

The game, though, ended in a 21–21 tie, the Cornhuskers' only blemish en route to the 1970 national championship.

"We all felt a lot of disappointment," Newton said. "We felt we should've won that game."

Not all was lost for Newton, though, as he mustered some sense of satisfaction in playing against the school he felt had stiffed him—the school that, at one time, was his dream.

"I do remember standing in the huddle and looking across the field in the second half and looking at John McKay," Newton said, "and I was thinking, 'Uh-huh, you could've had me. You could've had me.'"

Before Newton became a Cornhusker, when he was still a sophomore at Cerritos College, he remembers Devaney talking about some of the successful offensive linemen that had come through Nebraska. The name Bob Brown came up frequently.

"I remember Coach Devaney saying that Bob Brown was so strong that he could push a seven-man sled by himself. I never forgot that," Newton said. "I followed Bob Brown to Nebraska and had a very good offensive tackle career, also—not as good as Bob's, but I got some recognition."

The toughest player Newton ever played against was Herb Orvis, an All-American from the University of Colorado. The two, simply put, did not like each other. Orvis was a highly touted defensive end and Newton was getting notable publicity for his play at offensive tackle, and stories were written in the newspapers the week before the Cornhuskers and Buffaloes played, anticipating the duo's battle.

"We got after it pretty good," Newton said. "[People] sitting pretty high up in the stands, they could hear us colliding, our shoulder pads. He was the best college player I played against."

Orvis was a first-round NFL draft pick of the Detroit Lions. Newton was drafted in the third round by the Chicago Bears.

"We continued to play against each other for another three to four years in the same division in the NFL," Newton said. "The same dislikeness, the same competitiveness was carried all the way through into the NFL."

Newton had started lifting weights at Cerritos, so he was very committed to weightlifting. When Boyd Epley came on board at Nebraska, Newton worked out often with the Cornhuskers' new strength coach and developed a friendship. When Devaney and Nebraska really implemented a strength-training program, Newton felt he could overpower people because of the power and strength he'd gained from weightlifting.

Coaches also put players through what Newton remembers as a rigorous, gruesome winter conditioning program. One particular drill, called the Axe Drill, was designed to make players more aggressive. Devaney and assistant coach Cletus Fischer oversaw the drill.

"You'd go into the racquetball room and you had wrestling mats all over the floor and you would grab this axe handle," Newton said. "Coach Fischer would pair guys up. I'd only been in Lincoln about a week when we'd started this program, and I was exhausted by the time we got to this drill. He picked me and another guy, and the objective was to pull the axe, get the axe away from the other person—by any means. So he blew the whistle and I shoved this guy down pretty quick. I didn't get the axe away, but I had control of the drill pretty easily."

He'd gained control of the axe from Donnie McGhee, one of the starting offensive linemen.

"Everybody was excused, and Coach Devaney goes, 'Newt, I want you to stay here for a second.' Again, I was a new kid on the block. He said to me, 'You showed me a lot today, kid.' That's all he said. But he liked the aggression I had in the drill and that's what they were trying to get with this drill, to get the players more aggressive. That little inspirational talk I never forgot."

Devaney knew how to motivate. More specifically, Devaney knew how to motivate Newton.

"He would yell at me and scream at me," Newton said, "but he knew when to pull me aside and give me a compliment."

Nebraska's first home game of the 1970 Big 8 Conference season was against Missouri. The Cornhuskers won, but Newton had played a "really bad game," and he knew it.

"The next day we watched films, and after the films Coach Devaney grabbed me and said, 'Hey, Bob, do you want to play pro football when you're done here?' I said, 'Yeah, coach.' I wanted to go to the next level," said Newton, who, at that time, was highly ranked on draft boards.

"He said, 'Well, if you have another game like that, you might as well forget it.' He put it in that kind of tone, that seriously, and he just walked away."

The next week, Nebraska played Kansas in Lawrence, Kansas. The Cornhuskers won 41–20 and Newton was nominated by Nebraska's coaches for Big 8 lineman of the week. The talk from Devaney had served its purpose.

"Coach Devaney always had a keen sense of humor," Newton said. "He knew how to use humor with his players. He had good timing of when or what a player needed to hear or how to motivate that player. He had a temper. He could really get after you, but he didn't lose his temper all the time, so when he did lose it, you paid attention.

"When I was recruited I just felt he was someone I could trust and that he wanted me to be a part of getting the Nebraska football program back on board after those 6–4 seasons they had."

The turnaround began in Newton's first season, when Nebraska, obliterated at home by Oklahoma the previous season, shut down Steve Owens, who would win the Heisman Trophy that 1969 season, and beat the Sooners in Norman 44–14.

Owens had strung together 17 games of 100 rushing yards or more, and 16 straight games of at least one touchdown. Nebraska held Owens out of the end zone and to 71 rushing yards. The victory was Devaney's first in Norman, Oklahoma, and Nebraska also clinched a tie with Missouri for the Big 8 championship. The team celebrated as such.

"We threw Cletus Fischer into the shower," Newton said. "He was just going crazy, so a bunch of us just picked him up, threw him in the shower and showered him down. Just had a lot of fun, a lot of celebration after that game."

Why did the team single out Fischer?

"Everybody just really loved Cletus," Newton said. "He was just so happy. It was just out of fun and to enhance the celebration. It worked. Everybody cracked up."

Nebraska carried the momentum into a Sun Bowl victory over Georgia, and it helped set the tone for a 32-game unbeaten streak that included two national championships. Several players who played in the 1969 victory at Oklahoma also played in Norman two years later, and Newton said that taste of victory helped build confidence for the Cornhuskers' 1971 victory in the Game of the Century.

Newton didn't play in that historical game but he did play in Nebraska's first national championship game, a 17–12 victory against LSU in the Orange Bowl following the 1970 season.

Nebraska began that New Year's Day as the No. 3 team in the nation. Texas was No. 1 and began the day with a loss to Notre Dame in the Cotton Bowl. That essentially moved Nebraska to No. 2, still behind Ohio State, who would play in the Rose Bowl that afternoon. But the Buckeyes lost to Jim Plunkett and the Stanford Indians, leaving Nebraska as the only undefeated team in the nation, although the Cornhuskers did have the tie against USC on their record.

"I know we were on the bus going to the Orange Bowl, and I think it was announced on the bus, the score of the Ohio State game, and I can't remember the individual that announced it, but it was announced in that kind of format, where all of us knew we had a chance for the national championship," Newton said. "Coach Devaney just said, 'You win this game, you're going to be national champions.' That's what we had on the line. Everything fell into place to be in that kind of position to win a national championship that day."

LSU took a 12–10 lead in the fourth quarter, and Nebraska, behind quarterback Jerry Tagge, drove 67 yards for the go-ahead touchdown, with Tagge plunging in from the 1-yard line and stretching his arms over the pile.

"I just remember the confidence and the intensity of our huddle on that drive," Newton said. "It was very tense, and we knew what was on the line as far as the national championship, that we had to get the ball in the end zone to win it. The intensity and the confidence of play after play during that sequence of huddles, I remember that like it was last night. We were all so focused and we had to be, because we had to get the touchdown to win the national championship."

Or so Nebraska thought, anyway. Even after the Cornhuskers' 17–12 victory capped an 11–0–1 season, some controversy soon arose that perhaps Notre Dame should be voted No. 1 and win the national championship. The Irish had just defeated an undefeated Texas team, but had also lost to LSU earlier in the season.

The vote for No. 1 wouldn't come until the next day.

"I remember Coach Devaney, the next day when the newspapers came out, in the *Miami Herald* he had a huge quote in bold black that said, 'Even The Pope Can't Vote for Notre Dame to Be Number One.'"

Nebraska was indeed voted No. 1, receiving 39 first-place votes. Notre Dame finished second with nine first-place votes.

And Newton had concluded a successful, rewarding career at Nebraska, a career born in part because of a snub from his dream school.

"I've always had a great passion to play," said Newton, who played 11 seasons in the NFL. "That passion was really seeded at Nebraska, just the enthusiasm of the program and the phenomenal support from the fan base."

—Brian Rosenthal

CHAPTER 5

JOHNNY RODGERS

Wingback, 1969–72

Every great college football program has its iconic figures. These are the players every generation that comes after will remember, and their amazing stories become legendary. The University of Southern California has O.J. Simpson and Marcus Allen. Ohio State University has Archie Griffin and Eddie George. In the storied history of Notre Dame, it is arguable that Paul Hornung and Tim Brown exemplify that type of player. Nebraska's rival for many decades, Oklahoma, can easily place Billy Sims and Steve Owens on their list as well. For the Big Red, that list starts with a home-grown product out of one of Omaha's famed high schools, Johnny Steven Rodgers.

For Husker fans and foes alike, Johnny Rodgers is one of those athletes that can be referred to more by his nickname than the name that his parents gave him. Muhammed Ali is the "Champ." Red Grange was "The Galloping Ghost." Pete Maravich was "Pistol." In Nebraska, it's Johnny "The Jet." The Jet was a moniker he earned for his rapid acceleration and speed on the field.

In 1969, Johnny was voted high school athlete of the year as a player for Omaha's Tech High. Johnny's plan was to capitalize on that to reach his goal—to make $100,000 a year. In these days of multi-million-dollar contracts, $100,000 doesn't seem like a lot of money, but in those days, it was monumental. To a poor kid from the tough streets of Omaha's north side, that was more money than he could envision. He didn't even really know what $100,000 was; he just knew he wanted it.

So when Johnny was drafted to play for the Los Angeles Dodgers for $25,000 a year, it was a step in the right direction though nowhere near his dream. Fate, however, would play its part and Johnny Rodgers would not end up playing baseball. He would, instead, become one of the most decorated players in the history of the University of Nebraska and in all of football—and he would eventually make his $100,000-a-year paycheck and much more.

At the age of 17, Johnny went out to LA to spend a week with the Dodgers. He was met at the airport by his father, a man he had never met. Johnny didn't even know what his father looked like, so finding him at LAX proved difficult. On that fateful trip, his father, understanding Johnny's talents at football, pointed out that only three African American men had ever won the Heisman trophy. Two of them went to USC—"Tailback U." USC was winning championships and producing NFL players. Running back Ernie Davis of Syracuse was the first African American Heisman winner in 1961, followed by running back Mike Garrett in 1965 and running back O.J. Simpson in 1968. Garrett and Simpson came from USC.

It seemed to Johnny the path to $100,000 might be playing football at USC. Meanwhile, in Nebraska, Dick Christie, Johnny's high school football coach from Omaha Tech, and Charlie Washington, a mentor and civil rights activist in North Omaha, arranged a meeting between Johnny and University of Nebraska coach Bob Devaney. Upon Johnny's return from LA, he met with the now infamous coach. The meeting would end up framing the rest of Johnny's career.

Coach Devaney was smooth, complimenting Johnny's grandmother's cooking. Nonetheless, Johnny wasn't taking him too seriously. He likened Coach Devaney's looks to Mr. Potato Head. Nebraska had no championships, no pro players. Johnny was not interested in playing football for Nebraska. Nebraska was no Los Angeles Dodgers, and it was no USC. But Coach Devaney was smart, presenting Johnny with a deal he couldn't refuse. He offered a package deal: the possibility of Johnny pursuing his first love, baseball, at Nebraska if he agreed to play football for the Huskers as well. He also said that football might be a better route to that $100,000-per-year paycheck. Coach Devaney sweetened the deal by promising a massive draft effort to recruit African Americans and to win National Championships. In those days, there were not many African American players on any team.

Johnny couldn't refuse. He was excited about the opportunity to make a difference being part of the huge integration within college football of white and African American players. The promise of championships meant being part of a winning team, which positioned Johnny for the pros and that big payday. Being part of a winning team that didn't exist meant exposure and being a part of a new era in Husker football.

Coach Devaney was a man of his word. He recruited more African American players from high schools and junior colleges than ever, spearheading integration in college football programs. Johnny saw a winning team with Devaney creating All Americans and, in Johnny's sophomore year, they won a National Championship. Johnny's exposure was growing and he was truly earning "The Jet" nickname.

However, that year, smooth-talking Coach Devaney approached Johnny and asked him to concentrate solely on football and give up baseball. Johnny felt a bit like the coach was going back on a promise, but Devaney said he would create special plays to get him the ball and he would promote Johnny for the Heisman. Knowing Johnny's motivation, Devaney said it would increase Johnny's chance to eventually make that $100,000 a year. So again, with his goal in mind, Johnny took the deal. Coach Devaney was a man of his word, and in 1972 Johnny Rodgers not only won United Press International Offensive Player of the Year and the Walter Camp Award, but the Heisman Trophy. Johnny "The Jet" was on his way!

Johnny's respect and admiration for Coach Devaney was cultivated by Devaney's wisdom, foresight, and willingness to take risks. Devaney's racial integration and junior college recruitment set the model for many successful coaches in the future. But he was not the only Nebraska coach that fostered Johnny's success. Johnny boasts that all of the Nebraska coaches were world-class—they could have gone anywhere else and been head coach. Coach Tom Osborne, Johnny's position coach, provided extra tutelage and attention outside of regularly scheduled practice

Johnny Rodgers will always have some of the best seats at Memorial Stadium in Lincoln, Nebraska. (*Shelby Tilts of Shelby Suzanne Photography*)

throwing balls and running plays. When Coach Osborne called a play, the team just knew it would work, even if it sounded crazy.

Osborne would become one of the winningest coaches in college football history. He was inducted into the College Football Hall of Fame in 1999. Offensive line coach Cletus Fischer gave Johnny the green light to make his own plays and waive off the "fair catch." Johnny recalls Coach Fischer making him run stairs. Coach said, "Run them until you are tired. Then run them until I am tired!" Coach Fischer logged in 25 years leading Nebraska players and was inducted into the Nebraska Football Hall of Fame in 1979. Johnny was indeed coached by world-class coaches, becoming one of the best kick returners in college history.

Johnny admits the opportunities may have started with the amazing and invested coaches, but the true keys to his success were rooted in his teammates. "No one wins the Heisman alone. It truly is a team award," Johnny said. Middle guard Rich Glover was a hell of a blocker. Defensive end Willie Harper was fast. Jerry Tagge, quarterback, was a genius at play calling. Joe Blahak was one of the greatest and toughest blockers. Johnny recalls that even guys who didn't start were playmakers and leaders because the talent amassed was so great.

Johnny's favorite example of Husker teamwork came in the 1971 No. 1 Nebraska versus No. 2 Oklahoma "Game of the Century" on Thanksgiving Day. An estimated 55 million viewers, the largest TV audience for a football game at that time, watched Johnny run a 72-yard punt return for a touchdown. "You can't run if you have no blockers!" Johnny said. The biggest guy in the back of the field still ran to the end zone and made the last block to ensure the touchdown. "Nine blocks total in one play! No one gave up!" Johnny recalls. Johnny boasts that Richie Glover had a record 22 tackles in that game.

Nebraska beat Oklahoma 35–31 in this Game of the Century, giving the Cornhuskers a true national following resulting in sellouts at Memorial Stadium from 1962 to present day.

Rodgers' other true standout game might have been the 1973 Orange Bowl against Notre Dame. Two famous coaches, Devaney and Ara Parseghian, squared off as the Huskers were looking for a three-peat. Rodgers scored three touchdowns and caught a 50-yard pass for another score. He also threw a 50-yard pass to a teammate. The Huskers beat the Fighting Irish 40–6 as the Irish barely averted a shutout with a touchdown in the last few minutes. To Johnny, this was a memorable game in the highlight reels of his career, but to many it was a true testament to his talents and abilities. The 1973 Orange Bowl was Johnny's last collegiate game, and he played one for the history books. Rodgers left Nebraska with 5,586 total yards (6,059 with bowl games), a career average of 13.8 yards per touch, and 143 catches for 2,479 yards, 44 total touchdowns with 11 in one season, and 41 school records.

At the end of his career with the Cornhuskers, Johnny was drafted by the San Diego Chargers and offered $50,000, short of Johnny's goal. Sam Berger from Montreal's CFL Alouettes helped Johnny to realize that dream, offering him a $100,000 contract. He finally conquered his personal mission. Johnny's success continued and he became the CFL's Most Outstanding Rookie of the Year in 1973. He followed this up with CFL All-Star (1973–1975), CFL East All-Star (1973–1976) and Jeff Russel Memorial Trophy (1974–1975). His team won the 1974 Grey Cup championship. At this time in the early '70s, contracts were just starting to break the price barriers, and soon Johnny was making one million a year. In 1977, Johnny did join the Chargers after they picked up his CFL $1 million contract, but a freak knee injury ended Rodgers' NFL career after 17 games.

The results: 1972 Heisman winner, top pass receiver and kick returner in Big 8 history, *Sports Illustrated* 85th pick for the Player of the Century Team, ESPN pick for Top 25 Players in History, and a 2000 College Football Hall of Fame Inductee, just to name a few. Johnny's impact on Nebraska football, and all of football, is evident in the trail he blazed.

However, Johnny claims none of these are the real takeaway from his career at Nebraska. He said 20 years later, the real takeaway came in the form of a college degree—two, actually. He jokes that people would ask him when he would graduate to which he wittily replied, "When I am 50!" Johnny believes that "education is life" and now encourages other athletes, and all youth, to finish school. More than forty years later the scope and summary of his accomplishments for his era are astonishing.

Life after football, it appears, has been good to Johnny. Here are a few of his accomplishments, according to his official website:

- In 2005, he was named the University of Nebraska's Entrepreneur of the Year.
- In 2006, Johnny authored his first book, *An Era of Greatness: Coach Bob Devaney's Final Four Seasons in University of Nebraska Football (1969–1972)*, a must-read for all Cornhuskers fans.
- In addition to starting Rodgers Literary Marketing, Inc., Johnny is the founder of the Johnny Rodgers Youth Foundation. His program creates opportunities for youth through character, educational, and social development. Its partnership with the Network for Holistic Recovery allows at-risk youth to be exposed to wraparound services through a culturally competent network of case managers, service providers, and other resources in the community at large.
- During the last 10 years, Johnny has worked hand-in-hand with business leaders as a certified annual planning program facilitator for the Best Year Yet and Producing Results Systems. Johnny has developed a series of structured talks to help teams and organizations become masters at producing results.

Johnny is still in high demand as a public speaker. According to his website, "His inspirational talks encourage teamwork and persistence in reaching goals." Johnny regularly attends and assists events that support youth sports and leadership programs. He's active in Dr. Tom Osborne's Teammates Mentoring Program, as well.

Johnny was elected to the National Football Foundation and College Hall of Fame in 2000. The Sports Writers Association named Johnny the Most Valuable Player in Big 8 History. He's a member of the Nebraska Football All-Century Team, and in 2000 he was named the state's Husker Player of the Century.

In 2008, Rodgers was named to the Omaha Public School Hall of Fame, the *Sports Illustrated* Best Ever All-Time All-Star and the Orange Bowl All-Time team. CBS Sports named Rodgers number six on its list of Top 10 Players in College Football Ever.

For those of us who have followed "The Jet," we clearly can admire what Johnny has accomplished on the field as one of the best to ever play at Nebraska. However, we can also admire the fact that he has acknowledged his human failings that were widely reported in 1970. However and most importantly, he has never allowed that incident to define him.

According to public records, Johnny and two other men held up a gas station following a night of drinking. That chapter of his life has always been a silent asterisk in Johnny's accomplished career. Johnny has faced up to the mistake that he made on that day and led a life that allowed him to be granted a pardon from the state of Nebraska in November 2013.

"I feel like the weight for that particular incident is off my shoulders," Rodgers said after he walked out of his Board of Pardons hearing. As reported in the Associated Press, Johnny regrets the incident, which he admitted was an alcohol-fueled prank in the spring of 1970.

Rodgers expressed to the pardons board that he has tried to live a life that, while not perfect, can be an example to our youth that one mistake should not preclude you from becoming a productive member of the community. Johnny acknowledged, "I'm seeking a pardon because this incident happened when I was 17 years old. I had 10 minutes of insanity, which has hurt me my whole life." Osborne provided a letter of support. Johnny's story reminds us all that the good a person does should not be lessened by any mistakes that he may have made if he is willing to accept and seek redemption for those mistakes.

Johnny now lives in his hometown of Omaha. He is the vice president of new business development for Rural Media Group. He encourages youth, no matter what their situation, to surround themselves with the right people, mentors, and teachers—to study them and learn the path to success. Johnny looks back longingly at his "first girlfriend," baseball, but he has no regrets dumping her as the journey he took with the University of Nebraska Cornhuskers helped him to realize his goal of $100,000—and so much more.

—*George Achola*

CHAPTER 6

JOHN O'LEARY

I-back, 1972–75

If the University of Southern California is "Tailback U," then the University of Nebraska can make an equal claim to being "I-back U." To be a member of the Nebraska I-back club is to be a member of a club that has produced some of the most memorable moments in Nebraska football history. It is a club that produced some of the toughest athletes Memorial Stadium has ever seen. The names of its members roll off the tongues of any Nebraska fan: Rick Berns, Jarvis Redwine, Mike Rozier, Keith "End Zone," and Lawrence Phillips, just to name a few. They have come from every corner of the United States, ranging from New York to California. In the early 70s, a young man from New York was about to be a pioneering member of the I-back club.

In 1971, John O'Leary sat on the couch in his Long Island home and said to his dad, "I don't think I can play big-time football." Five winning coaches had visited John that week and he was questioning what to do. John's dad said, "What team just won two National Championships?" So John picked up the phone, called coach Bob Devaney at the University of Nebraska and said, "I am coming."

John stepped off the airplane in Omaha, Nebraska, not realizing that the state did indeed have more than one airport and he was at the wrong one. Lincoln and the University of Nebraska were an hour away, but Coach Devaney got John picked up and delivered to Lincoln for his first visit. John's first impression? There are, in fact, more than 30 people who live in Nebraska.

Being a New Yorker, John wasn't used to having a lot of friends, but he said, "Your friends are survival." John, known to be a tad wild and a bit of a prankster, quickly became close friends with fullback Jim Belka and kicker Rich Sanger. He also befriended quarterback Dave Humm, I-back Tony Davis, and defensive tackle John Dutton. John said guys like these made Nebraska feel like home. They became his companions— his family. John said, "We were all idiots, but we were close friends." He still recalls how the guys would go home with him to Long Island as they took turns visiting each other's families. The families, in turn, became close. They would meet up for a few games a year and all hang out together. The Husker family extended well beyond Nebraska.

The teammates and friends were close both off and on the field. John's close friend, Tony Davis, was "tough." John said Tony hit hard, blocked hard, and ran hard but thanks to Tony, John learned to never give up. They all wanted the same results. John said he never once walked onto the field thinking, "We aren't going to win," even against Oklahoma—and they never beat Oklahoma. John's biggest regret is never beating Oklahoma. He remembers the close games and said, "We should have beaten them."

In 1974, the No. 6 Huskers faced off against the No. 1 Sooners. Nebraska was tied 7–7 at the half and came out in the third quarter recovering a Sooner fumble. The Huskers could not capitalize on the fumble and the momentum was lost, resulting in an Oklahoma win 28–14.

In 1975, Nebraska struck first against Oklahoma and led 7–3 at halftime. The Huskers again came out strong in the third quarter and scored first after a Sooner fumble, creating a 10–3 lead, but Nebraska turnovers gave Oklahoma the edge. The Husker errors allowed Oklahoma to gain the upper hand. The Sooners took advantage of each turnover and scored, cementing a 35–10 Sooner win and Nebraska's first loss of the season. The Huskers were forced to share the Big 8 title.

Reminiscing about his teammates, O'Leary says I-back Dave Gillespie and fullback Tony Davis were just a few of the amazingly talented players with whom he shared the field. He says despite the individual talent, and despite the fact that all of them were very competitive, no one got caught up in themselves. Everyone contributed to the program.

John's most memorable game was Nebraska's disappointing loss to Wisconsin in 1974. Without starting quarterback Dave Humm, who was injured in the first quarter, Nebraska fell to the Badgers 21–20. John said in the first half of the game he was knocked hard and broke his jaw. X-rays didn't confirm or dispel a break, so they wired his jaw shut and he went back in. After another hit in the second half, the wires snapped. The trainers unwired his jaw, shoved a mouth piece in his mouth, rewired his jaw shut, and sent him back out. John was the Cornhuskers' offensive leader of that game, but the team lost and John was out the next three games.

Although playing with a broken jaw and being out for three games sounds horrible, John's least favorite memory was the 1974 Sugar Bowl. The No. 8 Cornhuskers played the No. 18 Florida Gators. While many will remember the Nebraska rally to win the game, saving themselves from humiliation in getting beat by a lackluster team, John doesn't remember a thing. He had a concussion early on and didn't see much playing time. He said he watched the film the following Monday and thought, "I don't remember any of that. I did that?"

Not one to despair, though, John healed and came back strong. His favorite win was the 1975 game against Miami, when a No. 4 Husker team trounced the Miami team. Miami tried to set the bar right off the bat as they scored two field goals and had a 6–0 lead. At the half, the Hurricanes were ahead 9–7 with the help of another field goal, but the Huskers took over in the second half. John bet a bottle of whiskey that the Huskers would get three touchdowns and Nebraska did not disappoint. The Huskers scored 24 unanswered points and John scored his bottle of whiskey.

Whether turning yards into points or touchdowns into booze, John was, and is, competitive. Two teams were his least favorite to play as a Husker: Colorado and Missouri. John said Missouri was the toughest, biggest and strongest. He said every win had to be earned. To the contrary, John claims Colorado was not "tough" like Missouri but they were very talented and put up a good fight. Colorado was fast, agile, and technical. Of course, John did enjoy playing a game like Kansas State when he would look down the bench and see the whiskey bottle out knowing the win should come easy. He would lean over to the crew and holler, "I'll be joining you in about 30–45 minutes!" John says it still feels rewarding that he was a starter with the level of talent he played with at Nebraska but he fully embraces the notion that no one, no coach or player, is bigger than the program.

While John made friends easily, he said the coaches were another story. John played for coaching legends such as Bob Devaney and Tom Osborne. Coach Devaney would ultimately have a Husker coaching record of 101–20–2 and would revive the Husker football tradition, bringing it and its talent to new levels. Coach Osborne would go on to become the winningest head coach in college football history with 25 years as head coach. John remembers that he and Coach Osborne did not get along, but he is still amazed at what he learned. John said the coaches were not his friends—they were coaches—but they all taught him to how to perform at his best.

Coach Jerry Moore shared with John a philosophy he still remembers—a player can have a God-given talent to run, catch, or throw, but it is the coaches that take that talent to the next level. He recalls how one of his favorite coaches, "Iron" Mike Corrigan, took him and fellow I-back Tony Davis to the roof of a building where a chalk line ran the edge. It was a long way down. Coach pointed at it and said, "We do not go out of bounds in Nebraska!" Looking over the edge of the building, the point was made. Until his retirement in 1982, Corrigan was the foundation for the toughness of Nebraska I-backs.

John recalls the now famous "Bummer-ooski" play against a tough Missouri team at Faurot Field. He was on the sideline and Coach Osborne told John to make the call. John said he knew his teammates would never believe him as he had a reputation for being a bit goofy at times. The nod from the coach confirmed it: activate the trick play! As chronicled in the *Lincoln Journal Star* the fake punt play came from assistant coach Jerry Moore, who brought it with him from his days at SMU. It was named after Bum Phillips who designed the play when he was a Bear Bryant assistant at Texas A&M. In 2013, the *Journal Star* broke down this play of Nebraska lore. What follows is a reconstruction of that play.

The punter, Randy Lessman, and Davis lined up closer to the line of scrimmage than normal, intentionally making the opponent think fake. The ball was snapped directly to Tony Davis, who stepped up and stuffed the ball between O'Leary's legs from behind. Davis then spun and faked a reverse to Monte Anthony to the right—Davis even yelled "reverse!" as a decoy. O'Leary, meanwhile, waited a couple of seconds in a crouch, acting as though he was going to be a blocker, before taking off unnoticed down the left side.

As O'Leary told the *Journal Star*, "The whole thing depends on deception. Their end came in and bumped me, thinking I was a blocker, but kept right on going after Anthony, who he obviously thought had the ball."

Players weren't supposed to look back at O'Leary, for fear of giving the play away. Tight end Brad Jenkins couldn't resist.

"Finally, I couldn't stand it any longer," Jenkins told the *Journal Star*. "But when I looked out of the corner of my eye, O'Leary was almost to the goal line."

Nebraska held a 10–7 lead in the second quarter when O'Leary's touchdown swung the momentum in a convincing 30–7 win. Davis said the victory was the most satisfying ever for him. John recalls that it completely changed the momentum of the game. That play laid the foundation for another famous Nebraska play a decade later: the "Fumblerooski."

Looking back and acknowledging he didn't always get along with the coaches, especially Osborne, John said as an 18-year-old kid out of Long Island, he didn't take anything too seriously. He admits to maybe having a little bit too much fun. He said he did mature during his time in Nebraska and learned a lot about being part of a team and contributing to a program, but in retrospect, he wished he would have been a little more serious and mature at the time.

Maturity eventually came, and John became a Husker I-back legend, capitalizing on his success being drafted by the Chicago Bears. The following year, he joined the Candian Football Legaue and played

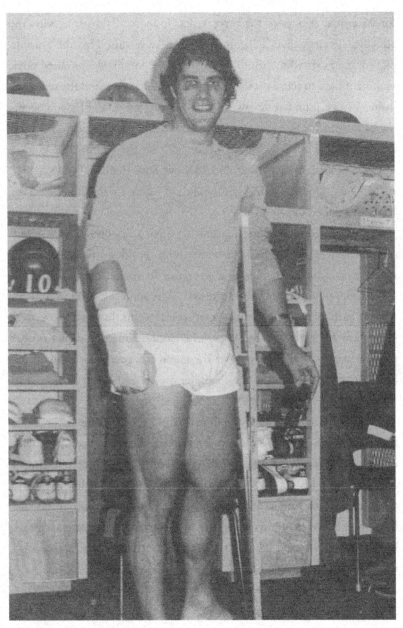

John O'Leary as a Montreal Alouette in 1977 with a broken nose, a broken wrist, and a sprained ankle after a game. (*Courtesy of John O'Leary*)

for Montreal Alouettes for three years. John recalls a game with the Alouettes against their Toronto rival, the Argonauts. He said Toronto played tough, smashmouth football. As proof, John had an injured nose, making it hard to see; a broken hand; and a hurt knee—and the team was losing 17–14. John barely saw his teammate, guard Doug Payton, walking out of the huddle through all of his swelling and sweat. John yelled to Doug, "You aren't helping!" Doug said, "Is the ball on the 45-yard line?" John said, "Yes." Doug said, "Do we have the ball?" John replied again, "Yes." Doug yelled, "I got them right where I want them!" and the Alouettes pulled out the win.

John's career in the CFL lasted for three years until a neck injury permanently halted his football career. John returned to Nebraska with his wife to raise his family, which eventually included three kids, six grandchildren, and another on the way. His son, T.J., followed in his father's path, playing for Nebraska on special teams. John said he understood how his parents felt going to the games, hanging out with other players' families as he now enjoys the game as a proud dad. John attributes his time at Nebraska for changing his life and he says he is proud to have played as a Husker.

John's success has followed him in his post-football career as he boasts $4 million in sales annually for a charitable gaming company with a territory covering six states. When asked when he will retire, he said, "I already have. I just haven't told anyone yet." The story of John O'Leary articulates how a simple decision has made all the difference in his life. Like the famous poem by Robert Frost illustrates, John came to a fork in the road of life, and he took the road less traveled. That has made all the difference.

—*George Achola*

CHAPTER 7

JERRY MURTAUGH,
SOPHOMORE YEAR

1968

Murtaugh's sophomore year would be his first season on the varsity team at Nebraska. His career seemed to get back on track after a turbulent freshman year, especially with his strong spring game, on a team that needed some defensive help after a 6–4 finish in 1967.

"The start of my sophomore year I had a talk with Devaney and there was only a little yelling," Murtaugh said. "So things seemed to be okay."

But there was a little incident—nothing major, according to Murtaugh.

"Now, I did have to visit the jail that year, but I got out on my own," Murtaugh said. "It was just an overnight thing."

However, he needed to go talk with the coach about an important life decision.

"I was set on getting married," Murtaugh said.

Devaney advised the college player against it.

"It had nothing to do with my potential wife," Murtaugh said. "He said don't marry her because your whole focus will change.

"I didn't take his advice and I got married."

Marital bliss was not something Murtaugh had a lot of, maybe thanks to his old pal Wally Winter.

Or thanks to Murtaugh, actually.

"My sophomore year I was married and lived off campus south of downtown Lincoln," Murtaugh said. "Wally Winter would bring beer over, and we would sit on the front porch and drink beer and just throw the cans on the front lawn."

Not everybody thought it was funny.

"My wife at that time was working afternoon shifts at a hospital," Murtaugh said, "and she would come home around 7:00 PM and see Wally and me sitting there in the front yard drinking beer, and she would get so upset with both of us.

"I would always blame Wally for bringing the beer over, but I was the one who always called Wally at his fraternity and said bring beer with you. To this day, my ex-wife doesn't like either one of us."

Jerry Murtaugh signs an autograph on Fan Day. Murtaugh would leave NU as the all-time tackles leader. *(Courtesy of Jerry Murtaugh)*

The team in 1968 would suffer, by Huskers standards, to a 6–4 record. They lost a number of close games. And late-season shutout losses to KSU at home (12–0) and Oklahoma on the road (47–0) did not leave Nebraska fans happy.

While the season did not have the desired results, Murtaugh said they had plenty of good players on a Huskers team that always seemed to be close to putting it together. Bowl-game appearances were not as plentiful in the late 1960s and while the Huskers had a winning record, it was not good enough to get to the postseason in 1968.

The standout players on the 1968 version of the Huskers started up front on offense with a big man, by 1960s standards: Joe Armstrong, at 6'1" and 225 pounds. He would earn All-American honors while playing offensive guard for the Huskers. The Beatrice, Nebraska, native was versatile—he was a backup punter in 1966, and in 1967 he played both guard and center.

Also on the offensive line was left guard Mel Brichacek, and Murtaugh said this offensive lineman kept it simple.

"Mel was one of the hardest workers on the team and never said much, but oh boy would he just hit you," Murtaugh said.

The defense probably had more standouts than the offense in 1968. Playing behind Murtaugh on the Blackshirt defense was a defensive back that was the complete package as a football player—and as a young man looking to enjoy the college co-eds of Lincoln, according to Murt.

"Dana Stephenson had any woman he wanted on campus," Murtaugh said of the All-Big 8 selection. "On the field he was a great player, he just had all the tools in a defensive back. He was smart, tall, and he could run fast. Also, he liked to hit you and to top it off, he had great hands and led the team in interceptions every year."

The linebacker playing alongside Murtaugh, Ken Geddes, would earn honors as well. Geddes, widely considered to be one of the best players to ever come out of Boystown High School in Omaha, was an All-American honorable mention in 1968. He earned All-Big 8 accolades as well that season.

The following year Geddes would repeat as an All-Big 8 selection by the coaches and media but at another position. Geddes, with his quickness and athletic ability at 6'3" and 235 pounds, was moved to middle guard on the defensive line. Many times Devaney called Geddes the best all-around athlete he ever coached. Geddes backed that up in the pros with an eight-year career with the Los Angeles Rams and the Seattle Seahawks in the NFL.

Being linebackers and guys who liked to hit things, Geddes and Murtaugh roomed together on the road. Of course, Murtaugh was not a good roommate.

"We roomed together on the road and I *really* did not know he didn't like snakes," Murtaugh said. "Just to goof around I put a fake snake in his bed one night, and I thought he was going to have a heart attack by the way he was screaming and running around.

"The coaches didn't like it, either."

Murtaugh would actually have more tackles than Geddes, with Murtaugh leading the team in takedowns in 1968, but both of them formed the backbone of the defense, which was the strength of the team. While the offense had good running backs in Joe Orduna and Dick Davis, the quarterbacks in 1968 would throw more interceptions than touchdowns. In fact, place kicker Paul Rogers would be the difference in three low-scoring wins in 1968.

Murtaugh himself would get his first postseason honors when he was selected Honorable Mention by the Big 8 conference that year. But maybe a bigger accomplishment for Murtaugh was staying off of Devaney's radar for the majority of his sophomore year, outside of the fake snake incident and the night in jail.

Unfortunately for the head coach, Murtaugh was just getting comfortable at Nebraska.

—Jimmy Sheil

CHAPTER 8

JIM PILLEN

Defensive Back, 1975–78

Tom Osborne did not utter the "D-word" lightly.

The year was 1978 and Sooner Magic was a young and vexing creature for Nebraska. It had been born two years earlier right where they stood. In 1976, the Sooners had been outplayed but used two trick plays to pull out an improbable victory and denied Osborne his first win over Oklahoma. The OU losing streak would become King Kong on the coach's back.

The coach, the stadium, and the state were starting to tighten up on the cold, November day.

The Sooners had been outplayed again and were behind late in the game to the Huskers 17–14. However, Oklahoma was driving with just minutes remaining in the fourth quarter with the Heisman winner-to-be Billy Sims gaining large chunks of yardage on play after play.

Sooner Magic was looking for oxygen to burn.

Adding to the bleak outlook was a break OU received minutes earlier when a Sooner fumble on a kickoff was missed by the refs. The "here-we-go-again" feeling was slowly enveloping Memorial Stadium as Oklahoma drove deep into Husker territory, and it looked like Osborne would lose his seventh straight game to the Sooners.

A timeout was called on the field. A senior captain and defensive back came to the sideline to talk to Husker defensive coordinator Lance Van Zandt.

An agitated Osborne joined the conversation.

"Some people probably had memories of two years earlier," said monster back Jim Pillen. "I was on the sideline and Lance was saying something and Coach Osborne came up and said, 'Daggum! We gotta make a play!'"

Pillen had an answer for the coach.

"Coach, don't worry; something good is gonna happen," Pillen said with no hesitation in 1978.

Almost thirty years later, Pillen echoed those thoughts.

A statue of Jim Pillen's coach, Tom Osborne, greets fans outside Memorial Stadium. Osborne changed Pillen's position on his first day of practice to monster back, where he would become All-Big 8. (*Shelby Tilts of Shelby Suzanne Photography*)

"There was not a shadow of doubt in our minds," Pillen said. "We believed someone would make a play."

Actually, two Huskers made plays.

Sims took a handoff at the NU 23-yard line and looked like a boxer smelling a K.O. The 6'1", 220-pound force of nature dashed and bullied his way inside the 5-yard line and was fighting for more yards when a Cornhusker made a jarring hit.

Huskers defensive back Jeff Hansen leveled Sims and caused a fumble. Pillen pounced on the loose ball and oranges would soon become projectiles in Lincoln, Nebraska.

Sports Illustrated was in town, writing about the next chapter in the already storied Huskers-Sooners series. Pillen talked to *SI* writer Douglas Looney after the game about Sims' last carry.

"I was running over, and the ball just popped up. Nobody was around it," Pillen said in the 1978 *Sports Illustrated* issue with running back Rick Berns on the cover along with the headline, "NEBRASKA BURSTS OKLAHOMA'S BUBBLE."

Maybe Osborne deserved the big play from Pillen for recruiting the lightly regarded major college prospect from Columbus Lakeview High School.

Even if it was late in the process.

"I didn't hear from Nebraska until Coach Osborne sent me a postcard from the Cotton Bowl around Christmas that year," Pillen said.

Pillen was considering colleges as signing day neared, but it did not consume Pillen. He had an older brother, Clete, who walked on at Nebraska and was in the process of earning a scholarship. Also, Pillen had a host of smaller college offers.

"I was working with my dad unloading some cattle and my mom yelled out that Coach Osborne was on the phone," Pillen said. "I was like, 'Sure, whatever, Mom.'"

"But coach was on the phone and he invited me down that weekend.

He ended up offering me a scholarship that weekend."

Osborne was looking at him for defense but Pillen had an offer to play offense, something usually more attractive to high school players. A native of David City, Nebraska, Pat Behrns, who would later coach football at University of Nebraska Omaha, was an assistant at New Mexico State at the time. Behrns liked what he saw at a skill position for Pillen.

"Pat said he thought I could be real successful as a running back and he asked me to visit," Pillen said. "I told Pat thanks, but I had my dream offer for college and I was going to Nebraska."

Osborne also had a hand in the position Pillen would play after he was originally put somewhere else as a freshman. At the time, the varsity head coach did not have too much to do with freshmen, unless possibly they were a quarterback or a running back.

"My third day on campus I was coming out early for freshmen practice after the varsity," Pillen said. "And I went by Coach Osborne and we each said hello to each other and we kept walking."

"But he took just a few steps and he came back and said, 'Jim, I see they have you at cornerback. Tell your coach today to switch you to monster back.'"

Pillen did that and played his whole career at monster back, a position that was basically a mix between strong safety and linebacker, a more physical position than cornerback. The coach's ability to project in an instant is still astounding to Pillen.

"Just how fast Coach Osborne could process in three steps for hundreds of guys was amazing," Pillen said. "Unbelievable. Brilliant."

The freshman team in 1975 was coached by Jim Ross. He had come to NU with Devaney in 1962, and many felt he was Devaney's top counselor. Pillen also felt he was the right guy to coach the freshmen as well.

"Jim Ross was a great father figure for us young kids," Pillen said. "He was the perfect guy to coach us. You felt you could go to him about anything as a wide-eyed freshman.

"With his wife in the ticket office, Mrs. Ross, they were like parents away from home for me. They took a liking to me for whatever reason and looked out for me. The Rosses were just a great Nebraska family."

On the scout team when the freshmen season was over, Pillen would get to know another Husker legend well. But this time the interaction would not be so pampering. The term "cremated" actually came to mind for Pillen.

"I would be on the scout team, and on goal-line defense, they would bump me up to linebacker," Pillen said. "We had Tony Davis, who was an extra physical fullback and he would have a good career in the NFL, too. So I would get low and try to take him on, but I would usually get cremated. Yeah, Tony was tough; his nickname fit him well.

"But that was the deal; you took your lumps and you got better."

The following spring, Pillen's first on varsity, the hard-hits would continue and Pillen did get better. This time he was probably on the giving end more as he moved up the depth charts on a team with about 150 players. By the end of spring ball, he was a close number two on the depth charter at monster back behind Ken Smith, who was a year older.

His defensive coordinator in 1976 was Monte Kiffin, who played at NU from 1959 to 1963 and began coaching for Devaney at Nebraska in 1966. Kiffin was famous (or infamous) for stealing a milk truck as a college student; his personality could run the gamut and he could be unpredictable. In one of Pillen's first varsity film sessions, the easygoing Kiffin showed he could get fiery quickly.

"Coach Kiffin is gently going over film at the start and maybe getting a little upset as we go along and getting a little louder at how well the offense was moving the ball," Pillen said. "But by the end of this film session, he was screaming and finally he took that 8mm projector and threw it against the concrete wall.

"And I thought, 'Geez what did I get myself into?' I think it is safe to say he used emotion more than Osborne."

The 1976 season would be significant for Pillen for two reasons. It would be his first year on varsity. Also, he would be playing on the same team with his brother, Clete.

"That was my senior year, and the possibility that both of us would be on the field at the same time was thrilling to think about," Clete Pillen said. "There wasn't always an awareness on my part when Jim was in the game. It was the responsibility of the strongside linebacker to get the defensive call to everyone in the huddle.

"After getting the call from the sideline and turning to the huddle to make the call, I would catch a glimpse of Jim in the huddle. What a sense of excitement it was to know we were on the field together. I know it was special for us, and our parents too."

Being brothers at different positions meant they didn't compete for playing time, but the brothers found ways to compete. Even at something as simple as a fitness run that all players needed to pass before the season started.

"As it turned out, the fitness run turned into a form of competition; we did so with the smallest of things," Clete said. "Each year, Boyd Epley, the strength and conditioning coach, would have everyone run six laps under 10 minutes around the 400-meter track that was just east of the stadium."

Part of the process of college football was conditioning, for better or worse.

"No one looked forward to the agony; heck, it was football, not track," Clete said. "Since Jim and I worked out together, we decided to run the mile and half together.

"Off we went at a nice pace but the closer we got to that final lap, we could sense the competitive juices [were] flowing."

And big brother had a plan.

"Jim ran the 100 meters in track and a 40 at 4.5, so I decided if I was going to beat him that on the last lap I had to sprint," Clete said, laughing. "Jim thought I would never last as I broke into sort of a sprint to the finish line."

But being brothers meant they would look out for each other as well.

"I lost my mouthpiece one time on a punt and I'm on the sideline wondering where the heck it was on the field and then Jim walks up with it," Clete said. "Not a huge thing, but it was him being a brother and watching out for me when he wasn't in the game."

The 1976 Huskers came into the season with high expectations and were the preseason No. 1 team. They had started the previous season 10–0 and lost two games to end the year. Nebraska could have won both games since they held leads in the second half of both contests.

They led Arizona State 14–6 going into the fourth quarter before falling in the Fiesta Bowl 17–14 in a quasi-home game for the Sun Devils. They did lose to Oklahoma 35–10, but an early third-quarter touchdown had NU leading 10–7 before a series of miscues allowed the Sooners to run away with the game.

Expectations were so high in part because of the return of the Big 8 Newcomer of the Year in 1975 in senior quarterback Vince Ferragamo. He was a newcomer in the Big 8 as a junior in 1975 as Ferragamo transferred from Cal University after being behind an older player in future All-American Steve Bartkowski, a future NFL player.

Pillen knew from day one that they had a player in the dark-haired Italian.

"Immediately with Vince in practice it was like wow! He could make throws nobody else could," Pillen said of the signal-caller who would join Bartkowski in the NFL and have a successful career too.

The Huskers opened the season in 1976 versus LSU with a tie at maybe one of the toughest places in the country to play, at the Tigers' stadium in Baton Rouge, Louisiana. However, NU dropped to No. 8 in the polls. Also, a few Big 8 losses kept them out of the national championship picture, but with no dominant Big 8 team in 1976, the Huskers were in the Big 8 race until the end of the season.

Nebraska and Oklahoma would meet in 1976 with the winner getting a share of the Big 8 championship. The Huskers, playing at home, would be favored. This year was a watershed year because it started a trend of OU pulling out late and dramatic victories, usually with a big play that NU fans would not soon forget.

"We had a better team in 1976 but they beat us with [hook-and-ladder] and halfback pass," Pillen said. "And Sooner Magic was born. That was tough because we had a really good team and just how it happened."

NU led 17–7 going into the fourth quarter. But Oklahoma used two trick plays to pull out a 20–17 win. In fact, those two plays were actually the only Sooners passes of the game. The name Elvis Peacock stills makes people in Nebraska sigh deeply.

With the score 17–13 late in the fourth quarter, Sooners quarterback Dean Blevins completed a pass to an OU receiver. Then the receiver pitched the ball to Peacock, who took it to the 2-yard line on the Sooners' hook-and-ladder play. Oklahoma punched it in the end zone with 38 seconds left to beat Nebraska, despite Clete recording 27 tackles on the day.

The loss to Oklahoma in 1976 was painful not only because of how it happened, but also because it kept Nebraska from a share of the Big 8 championship. At 4–3 in the Big 8, the Huskers finished in a tie for second behind three teams—Oklahoma, Colorado, and Oklahoma State University—with a 5–3 conference record, and Colorado went to the Orange Bowl.

After the Oklahoma game, in a scheduling move made occasionally at the time, the last game of the regular season was at Hawaii. On the Big Island, the often surprising Kiffin showed his unpredictably again.

"At the end of the year we beat Hawaii and we were up like 50–2," Jim Pillen said. "And late in the game Mike Fultz [a 300-pound defensive tackle] asked if he could play some defensive back and Kiffin sent him in the game. Mike is playing free safety out there doing the aloha dance, waving his arms and legs like a Hawaiian dancer. It was funny!

"But Devaney was pissed off after the game in the locker room at him for doing that. Kiffin could do some interesting things."

The 1976 season was capped off with a come-from-behind win in the Bluebonnet Bowl over Texas Tech. Clete remembered it was Osborne, and not Kiffin, who was animated at halftime and got them going to rally for the win over the Red Raiders. Pillen finished the season with 13 tackles and an interception.

Having his brother graduate was not the only change for Jim for the 1977 season. The other change might have given him the edge in overtaking Smith, a senior, for the starting job.

Kiffin left for Arkansas and in came new defensive coordinator and defensive backs coach Lance Van Zandt. Van Zandt felt two things were important for his players—the ability to hit…and the ability to hit.

"In 1977 Lance Van Zandt's goal was to start the 11 toughest, hardest-hitting players on defense," Clete said. "It was last man standing got the job, if you will."

The older brother knew his younger brother would thrive in Van Zandt's defense.

"Jim would not back down from any challenge; he is a true example of a competitor," Clete said.

The younger Pillen didn't speak so dramatically about the situation. He sounded more relieved to leave Nebraska above ground.

"Playing for Lance almost killed me," Pillen said, smiling. "He wanted physical DBs and I was probably the most physical, so I got the nod in 1977."

While Jim was a physical player, another teammate of Pillen's mentioned another attribute of the Columbus native that helped Jim to displace a senior starter.

"Jim would hit you no question, but more than other guys he was smarter with the way he played; he was analytical," said Oudious Lee, a defensive lineman at the time. "Jim was in the right place at the right time. Great instincts."

Pillen was in the right place at the right time in 1977 versus Alabama. Pillen's older brother said he prepared well for that game by studying individual players.

"I remember Jim saying after the game that in the game Ozzie Newsome showed some tendencies when running his route," Clete said. "Also, what he saw in preparing for the game on film made it clear to him when to step in front of that last pass thrown by [Jeff] Rutledge.

"Jim was a student of the game, which clearly showed why he earned the academic honors that he did," Clete added.

As was his nature, Pillen, the two-time Academic All-American, downplayed his performance and broke down the Alabama game in simpler terms.

"I was cheating on Ozzie because he was their best player," Jim said, "so I figured they would be looking for him."

The Alabama win followed a surprising home-opening loss to Washington State, now coached by former Huskers assistant coach Warren Powers. He was Jim Pillen's position coach at Nebraska, as well.

The topsy-turvy season continued for NU in 1977 as the Huskers broke in a new quarterback in Tom Sorley. However, a few good I-backs along with an improving Sorely at quarterback kept Nebraska in the Big 8 race. The tandem of I.M. Hipp and Berns meant NU had two horses with differing styles that opponents had to contend with on Saturdays.

"Hipp was awesome," Pillen said of the player who would go from a walk-on to an All-American. "He could make you look bad because he had so much wiggle and he was elusive as a runner."

Berns was a unique running back, as well.

"Bernsy was a tall and fast guy who was quick and you had to get after him to tackle him," Pillen said. "He was a load to try to take down so you had better be in good position with him."

A midseason conference loss for Nebraska in 1977 meant an undefeated Oklahoma had the championship wrapped up before the rivalry game. And no late-game heroics by OU were needed anyway as they cruised to a 38–7 win over the Cornhuskers. By the end of the year, Pillen justified the promotion by leading the defensive backs in tackles and finishing third on the team in tackles, with 79, behind linebacker Lee Kunz and defensive end George Andrews.

The 1977 season was Pillen's first with new defensive coach Charlie McBride. His temperament was in some ways like Van Zandt in terms of getting his team ready for physical play.

"During practice, Coach Osborne might go to the other end of the field," Pillen said, "and Charlie would maybe look around and say, 'We're going live!' And we would get after it pretty good until Osborne came back."

McBride also noted Pillen's style on the field.

"Jim was tougher than mustard gas," McBride said. "When you-know-what hit the fan, Jim would show up and he bailed us out a number of times, like his interceptions versus Alabama. He was an outstanding leader for the Blackshirts and he was respected by all his teammates.

"His parents brought him, and Clete, up right too. If I ever had to go to battle, I would want those boys with me. Their dad too."

McBride's first NU season wrapped up the season with a bowl win. Backup quarterback Randy Garcia would relieve Sorley and lead a comeback. In fact, after the Liberty Bowl victory over North Carolina, Osborne was now 4–1 in bowl games since taking over the team in 1973.

But as Pillen and NU prepared for the 1978 season, Nebraska fans were wanting more than bowl wins versus good-not-great teams and second-place Big 8 finishes.

That opportunity to take Nebraska to the next level and appease Husker fans would present itself with the Oklahoma game in 1978. But this was a better-than-usual OU team, which was usually outstanding anyway. They came in undefeated and ranked No. 1 with only a few close calls with the wishbone attack led by quarterback Thomas Lott and running back Billy Sims.

Pillen knew the Huskers were underdogs in most people's eyes, but not their own.

"Nobody gave us a chance versus Oklahoma in 1978," Pillen said, "but we believed we could beat them. You have to believe you have a chance."

"We just played good team defense and we hit them and hit them."

Hit them they did as OU fumbled nine times, losing six. Pillen actually recovered another fumble but a penalty on Nebraska wiped it out. The last fumble recovery set in motion a crowd reaction common at the time in the Big 8.

"We request that boys and girls do not throw oranges on the playing field," the public address announcer at Memorial Stadium said as fans began to toss oranges on the field. The Huskers faithful were getting ready to let loose as Nebraska was in the driver's seat for multiple goals that had been eluding them since 1971.

Osborne talked to *Sports Illustrated* after the game about maybe where the "daggum" came from.

"I know of the grumbling that I can't win the big one and I can't beat Oklahoma," Osborne said in the locker room to *SI* writer Looney. "I knew I better beat them pretty soon."

He went on in the 1978 interview to jokingly talk about his public perception.

"I guess some people think of me as a stick in the mud," Osborne said.

Osborne had a momentary smile, but thanks to a scheduling quirk, the conference season was not over for the Huskers. For the first time since 1959, Nebraska would not finish the conference season playing Oklahoma.

NU would play a good Missouri team in Lincoln. Also, the new coach at Mizzou was Powers, the former Huskers assistant and player who had beaten Nebraska the previous year as coach at Washington State.

Powers was an assistant at Nebraska until 1976 and he was Pillen's position coach as well. Pillen noted Powers was a coach who often had more complex schemes on defense than others in the 1970s.

Whether it was Powers' schemes or the fact that Nebraska was recovering from a physical game with Oklahoma—or that the Tigers were just better that day—Mizzou won a back-and-forth game. The 35–31 loss was an especially tough result for Pillen to deal with as a senior.

"Missouri had a lot of good players and no shame there," Pillen said. "But it has taken me 25 years to get over that game because we were the better team and we lost a shot at the national championship. And I could have played better.

"But we were physically beat up after the Sooner game and they just made more plays in the end."

Pillen did play well but the NU defense as a whole struggled to stop an all-conference-caliber running back in James Wilder, along with future NFL tight end Kellen Winslow. The future Pro Bowl running back would have 181 yards rushing and score four touchdowns. NU's Berns had a career day with 255 yards rushing, but Wilder's late touchdown was the difference.

But not all was lost, as the Cornhuskers were still co-Big 8 champions with Oklahoma, Osborne's first of many conference titles. However, fate still had one more twist in store for Osborne.

With the other national results that Saturday, the Orange Bowl lost a national championship game and one of the highest-ranked remaining teams for them to choose was Oklahoma. Pillen's dad, Dale, was in the locker room shortly after the Missouri game as Osborne got off the phone with bowl officials.

The coach asked Pillen's father to step in his side office for a moment.

"So my dad goes in this little office in the hallway," Pillen said. "And Coach Osborne said to my dad, 'I just got off the phone with the Orange Bowl and they are telling us we are playing Oklahoma again.'"

Jim Pillen was elected to the Board of Regents for the University of Nebraska in 2012. *(Courtesy of the University of Nebraska)*

Mr. Pillen had a suggestion for Osborne.

"So my dad says, 'Call them sons of bitches back up and tell them to go to hell!'" Pillen said, laughing.

Osborne did not do that. Instead he took it the best way he could and started preparing for Oklahoma.

The team he had just beaten.

The team to which NU had lost six times in a row.

The team, and the game, that had become almost a noose around his neck.

A loss to Oklahoma in the Orange Bowl might take some of the hard-earned luster off the recent milestone win, co-Big 8 champs or not. Now Osborne was playing Oklahoma and coach Barry Switzer in an almost unheard of intra-conference bowl matchup just over a month later.

In the rematch, Sims was looking for more than the victory after his fumble at the end of the previous game was basically the clincher for the Huskers. Sims took out some of his frustration during the Orange Bowl when he had a clear path to the end zone on a run but waited for a Nebraska defender—not Pillen—and plowed him over on his way to six points. Sims would end up with MVP honors in the game, as well.

The out-for-revenge Sooners won the rematch in the Orange Bowl 31–24, in Pillen's last game as a Cornhusker. While the first half was close, the Sooners held a two-score to three-score lead for most of the second half. NU did tack on a touchdown as time expired.

Pillen's career was about as decorated as a player's could be while rarely touching the ball, or making sacks like a lineman, or racking up as many tackles as a linebacker. He was a two-time All-Big 8 pick and a two-time Academic All-American. He was inducted into the Nebraska Football Hall of Fame in 2004, and he secured turnovers late in two games that were among Osborne's biggest wins in the 1970s (Alabama 1977, Oklahoma 1978).

But his older brother said those things happened because Jim was a team player first.

"Jim will be the first to tell you that it's not about him, it's about the team," Clete said. "It takes an entire team to accomplish the goals established each year. It's all about building the team chemistry, which starts with each player on the team and everyone's sacrifice."

Jim Pillen passed on a pro career, even though the Dallas Cowboys told him they were going to draft him in the later rounds. He felt he needed to be completely focused to be a successful pro and by the spring of 1979 he had been accepted to veterinarian school, a difficult placement. Pillen knew his graduate school spot might not be there in two or four years after professional football.

He attended vet school at Kansas State and graduated in 1983.

His post-football days have been similar to his football days in terms of the company he keeps. He runs and owns Pillen Family Farms with Clete in Columbus, Nebraska, a business founded by their dad. Pillen Family Farms is a farming company with a focus on raising pork while protecting the environment and promoting animal welfare.

The All-Big 8 defensive back stays in contact with Osborne through the coach's foundation, TeamMates, which provides mentors for teens. TeamMates is just one of many non-profits Pillen has volunteered for in the state of Nebraska. The Columbus native is a board member for Osborne and has done that for many organizations in the last few decades.

Pillen has served as the chairman of the board for the Columbus Community Hospital, the Scotus Central Catholic High School Endowment Board, and the Columbus Area Chamber of Commerce.

He has also branched out into politics, and predictably, it involved the University of Nebraska. In 2012, Pillen was elected to the Board of Regents for the University of Nebraska system. The Board of Regents supervises the operations of the university system and oversees all expenditures.

Some necessary skills for a University of Nebraska Regent are to be detail-oriented, thorough, and probably a bit cautious, too. Pillen showed this maybe to an extreme in the aftermath of his biggest play as a Husker.

"After the fumble recovery with Sims, I was just standing there holding the ball and showing it to the official, double-checking with him," Jim Pillen said, laughing. "I wanted to make sure it was finally our ball after the fumble on Ruud's hit was missed and it was *really* our ball."

—*Jimmy Sheil*

CHAPTER 9

MITCH KRENK

Tight End, 1978–82

The first play of the game had already been scripted.

Nebraska coach Tom Osborne normally opened the Corn-huskers' first series with a simple dive or pitch play, but against unranked Oklahoma State on November 7, 1981, in Stillwater, Oklahoma, he had a different strategy. Osborne had planned a fake iso to running back Mike Rozier. Tight end Jamie Williams would initially block, then slip downfield, free to receive a pass from quarterback Turner Gill. While nothing terribly fancy, such a passing play from Osborne's conservative playbook could be regarded as a trick play.

"I knew the first play was a really awesome idea," said Mitch Krenk, another Cornhuskers tight end who'd played primarily in double-tight-end situations. He also served on special teams, notably kickoff returns.

Krenk, a junior from Nebraska City, Nebraska, was on the field as the Cornhuskers received the opening kickoff. When the play was finished, Krenk was jogging toward the sideline when he looked up and heard coaches yelling at him to get back in the game. Krenk looked back. Williams lay on the ground, holding his knee.

Thoughts quickly raced through Krenk's head, the first of which was about the trick play he knew Osborne had ready to run. With Williams out, Krenk was the next man up.

"I'm like, 'I'm going to get this play, man!'" Krenk said.

Indeed he did. Just like the play was designed, Krenk slipped down-field, got open, and caught Gill's pass. Had Krenk been blessed with more speed, he believes he would've scored. "But some DB caught me." As it was, the play gained 35 yards.

That's when Krenk began to blossom. He caught three more passes that day, including one for a 9-yard touchdown, and finished with 53 receiving yards in No. 11 Nebraska's 54–7 romp of the Cowboys.

Years later, Krenk learned the true story behind the calling of that play, from an assistant coach at the time, Gene Huey.

"He was always on the headset with Osborne during the game,"

Krenk said. "He said Jamie got hurt, and he said, 'I told Coach Osborne to go ahead and run that fake iso pass.' He said Coach Osborne said, 'But … Mitch is in there.' Of course he tells me, 'Oh, Mitch can do it, he does it in practice.'

"That's so typical of coaches. They don't really trust you until you do it in a game. You can do it in practice, do it in practice, but they don't ultimately trust you until you do it in a game. Fortunately for me, that game, I had a really good game. Then it was like Coach Osborne trusted me now."

Fast-forward a year later. Nebraska is hosting rival Oklahoma, and the Cornhuskers are running the football successfully against the Sooners. Osborne grabs Krenk to send in the next play. Krenk doesn't remember the exact name of the play, only that the words "bounce pass" were somehow included.

"I told Turner, 'We're running such-and-such bounce pass,' and Dave Rimington goes, 'We're not running that goddamn fucking play!' He was pissed. He wanted to run the ball, and it only worked about half the time in practice," Krenk said. "I said, 'Dave, man! I'm just the messenger!'"

Here's why the play rarely worked: it was risky. Gill would intentionally bounce a pass in the flat to wingback Irving Fryar, who would sort of ease up, conning the defense into thinking he'd just picked up an incomplete pass before firing downfield. The trickiest part of the trick play, naturally, was the bounce, but that part of the play worked flawlessly that day at Memorial Stadium.

"So we run the play, and I still remember I block the guy, and I'm running downfield, and I think it was Scott Case, who ended up playing in the NFL as a great safety, and he was right on my hip," Krenk said. "I turn back, and Irving Fryar—Coach Osborne told him, 'If [Krenk is] even close to covered, you just run it. Get what you can and run it.'"

Fryar had no time to sell the "incompletion." An Oklahoma defender was right in his face. So instincts took over.

"He frickin' throws it," Krenk said.

Krenk compared it to the catch kids make with their buddies in the backyard, just jacking around. Only this was on Senior Day, his last game ever at Memorial Stadium, against rival Oklahoma.

"I kind of got a finger on it, came back, caught the ball," Krenk said. "Scott Case clocked me pretty good."

The play, later famously named "The Bouncerooski," gained 37 yards early in the second quarter and set up a touchdown in Nebraska's 28–24 victory, sealed by Scott Strasberger's interception, which sent students pouring onto the field.

That night, Krenk was at his trailer house on West A Street in Lincoln when he happened to think he'd better check the local television news for highlights of his play. Sure enough, they showed it, but that got Krenk thinking—could this be big enough to make that big national network, ESPN? He had cable, and turned to the relatively new all-sports channel. Chris Berman was narrating highlights.

"They go, 'Nebraska-Oklahoma...' [and] I'm getting all excited," Krenk said. "Then he says, 'Coach Osborne reaches in his bag of tricks.' Holy shit, they're going to show it! So Chris Berman in his voice says, 'Turner Gill, bounces the ball out to Irving Fryar, who throws it downfield to...a tight end.'

"I remember thinking, you know what? I'm a walk-on, man. They don't even know my name on there. I was feeling so good...and feet back on the ground."

Krenk, something of a late bloomer at Nebraska City High School, was a walk-on in practically the literal sense. At age 18, he walked into the Nebraska football coaches offices one late summer day in 1978, unannounced.

"I went up to the second floor, where the coaches' offices were, and I asked the secretary if I could see Coach Osborne," Krenk said. "And she says, 'Do you have an appointment?' I'm like, 'Well, no, should I come back? I just drove from Nebraska City.' She goes, 'Oh, you drove from Nebraska City? Let me see.'

"She calls back there, and here comes Coach Osborne walking down the hallway. I said, 'Hi, coach, my name's Mitch Krenk from Nebraska City.'"

Krenk came prepared to answer questions about his vertical, his 40 time, and his bench press. He'd been working at a local grocery store after graduating from high school and thought he might go to Peru State to play on a small scholarship. Until that May, he'd never lifted free weights, only some universal machines in gym class. But a local Pepsi driver owned a York Olympic weightlifting set and began working with Krenk.

"We were doing bench three times a week, 15 sets a day," Krenk said. "Every weekend, we'd max out, and every weekend, my max was going five, 10 pounds higher."

By the time Krenk headed to Lincoln that day on a whim, he was benching 295 pounds and had increased his body weight from 185 to 200 pounds. He stood at 6'3". He figured he at least resembled a football player in the presence of Osborne, although the coach never asked how fast Krenk could run, or how much he could lift, or if he could see any film.

"He kind of looks at me and says, 'Well, how are your grades?' I said, 'Well, I'm a pretty good student, coach. I get A's and B's, once in a while a C.' He goes, 'Okay, are you enrolled in school?' I remember I told coach, 'No, but I will be if you let me walk on.'"

Osborne pulled out a little piece of paper, gave it to Krenk and told him to go see a man named Walt, the equipment guy for the freshman team, and to report on a certain day.

"I walk out of there going, 'Holy crap! I'm walking on!'"

Krenk enrolled in school and reported for the first day of practice for the freshman team, which would play four or five games under coach

Guy 'The Fly' Ingles. Krenk soon discovered he wasn't the only fresh-man Osborne allowed to walk on. Some 150 newcomers arrived that first day, although Ingles announced after two practices that number would have to be cut to less than 100. The list included scholarship players like Jimmy Williams and Bruce Mathison. The only freshman not there was Rimington, who'd already been placed on varsity.

Krenk thought himself to be a linebacker, but found himself in a group with 35 linebacker wannabes.

"Krenk!" barked out Ingles, who certainly didn't know Krenk but saw his name written boldly in magic marker on athletic tape across his helmet. "Hey, Krenk! You ever play tight end?'" Krenk said he did in high school a little bit, "but I think I would be a good linebacker, coach.'

"He's like, 'Well let me tell you something. See those two guys right there?'" He pointed to Jamie Williams and Dan Hill, both on scholar-ship. "He goes, 'That's my two tight ends. I have no walk-on tight ends.' I go, 'I'm a tight end!'"

Krenk saw significant action on the freshman team that season. He kept lifting, and even broke the Nebraska tight-end bench-press record, which was 295 pounds, held by Junior Miller. Krenk put up 300, which at the time was Osborne's goal for his offensive linemen. That sparked Krenk's confidence heading into winter conditioning in the old mush-room gardens in the bowels of East Stadium.

There were two groups for winter conditioning—scholarship play-ers and other main contributors with strength coach Boyd Epley and his assistants, and everybody else in what was called the dirt group. Krenk was in the latter.

"I didn't have any coach that really recruited me or anything, so I didn't have anybody who was like my advocate. So I was in the dirt group," Krenk said. "We were down there jumping rope in the dirt, doing up-downs in the dirt, and then running around that freaking track. That's where we did winter conditioning."

Toward the end of winter conditioning, Krenk one day noticed about five varsity coaches come down and watch the dirt group. That was a red flag for Krenk. Although he'd already been "busting his butt," he picked it up a notch in the presence of the coaches. Not everybody did that, and Krenk couldn't figure out why.

"After winter conditioning, they brought us all together, 30 or 40 guys down there," Krenk said. "They go, 'You and you. You guys stay. Everybody else can go.'" Krenk was one of the two who could stay and earned an invitation to spring practices. The rest were finished.

The number next to Krenk's name on the spring ball depth chart was in double digits, but coaches kept him around. Over the next couple of years, he kept getting bigger and stronger in Epley and Mike Arthur's strength program. He moved into the varsity locker room and earned a real jersey, No. 89, which had been worn by Miller.

Practices weren't easy. Huey, in Krenk's opinion today, was a great receivers coach. But at the time, Krenk couldn't stand him.

"He ended up being the coach I hated," Krenk said. "I was always, 'Why the hell is he always picking on me?' He would make me go during group work and George Darlington would be yelling, 'Krenk! Come over here! Krenk! Come over here! Get down here!' And I'd have to go block those guys by myself the whole time. Then Huey was always on my ass."

"Looking back, they saw something. I remember asking Darlington one time, 'Why'd you guys always pick on me, man? Dan Hill and Jamie Williams were running little pass routes and shit, and I'm getting my head knocked down by George Andrews.' He was like, 'Well, you gave us a really good picture, that's why we had you come down there.'"

Andrews and Derrie Nelson, in particular, would just "beat the crap" out of Krenk.

"George Andrews, they'd call him the Smiling Assassin. That was his nickname. And it was true," Krenk said. "He would club me across the head and make the play, and then he'd come over and help me up, [and say], 'Good job, Mitch. Good job.'"

Going against those guys helped Krenk realize he'd finally arrived, though, during his sophomore season.

"I go to a party down in the Bottoms, and I go to this house, and there's some varsity guys. Derrie Nelson and David Clark—mean guys, really tough players—Dan Pensick. They were back around the keg. They said 'Hey! There's that Krenk kid! Come on over here!'

"You know what they said? They're like, 'Man, you're going to be a player. You bring it every day, you do this and that.' It really made me feel good to have these varsity guys say that about me."

The spring leading into his junior season is when everything came together. Krenk performed well in the Spring Game and moved ahead of Hill for the No. 2 spot, behind the No. 1 man, Williams. That's when Krenk remembered Osborne's rule—any player who rose as high as No. 2 on the depth chart as a walk-on earned a scholarship. It's why Krenk became excited when he was summoned into Osborne's office.

"He says, 'Well, Mitch, you've done really good, but dagummit, I just don't have a scholarship available,'" Krenk said. "I go, 'What do you mean, coach?' He said, 'We're going to give you one at semester.' I go, 'Coach, Dan Hill's been on scholarship for three years, and I'm ahead of him, I've paid my own way for three years, why don't you take his away?!' Coach Osborne goes, 'Well, Mitch, we just don't do it that way here.'"

By the following spring semester, Krenk was on scholarship. That came after Nebraska's 9–3 season, the one in which Krenk had his breakout game at Oklahoma State and a season that ended with a loss to national champion Clemson in the Orange Bowl.

That set the stage for his senior season and famous "Bouncerooski" play—both of which almost didn't happen.

Krenk was running a pass route during a practice of his final spring ball season when he felt a pop in his foot—a really, really painful pop. He removed his shoe, then his sock, and saw his middle toe flopping around. "I freaking broke my toe!" Krenk remembers.

X-rays showed what resembled a honeycomb at the end of the bone of his toe. Believing it was decalcified bone or necrosis, doctors advised removing the end of his toe, saying Krenk would heal in time to return within a week or two. Krenk had the procedure and was back on the practice field in less than a week.

Not long after that, Krenk was at the training table, then at Selleck Quad, eating lunch with the guys. Some woman, perhaps one of the cooks, entered the room and loudly asked if there was a Mitch Krenk in the room. Krenk raised his hand.

"You need to go to Coach Osborne's office," the woman said.

Krenk, after getting ribbed by his teammates, walked over to Osborne's office, trying to recall all of the stupid stuff he had recently done, wondering which of his acts had gotten him in trouble with the head coach.

"I walk in there, and I'm not lying," Krenk said. "Coach Osborne is as white as a ghost. Right then I thought something happened to my parents or family. My mind just went, 'Uh-oh, this ain't good.'"

Osborne told Krenk to have a seat, and he began talking about the procedure that had removed Krenk's toe. Krenk said he was feeling fine.

"He goes, 'Well, the pathology report came back, and it's Ewing Sarcoma. That's cancer.'"

What?

"I go, 'Well, they got it, right?'"

Osborne was quiet.

"Mitch, this is serious. You need to talk to the doctors."

He did, immediately, and the doctors were blunt. This was a blood-traveling cancer, usually in a larger bone, like a femur, shoulder, or back. The fact this was in a secondary location greatly concerned them. They told him of a man in Lincoln who'd had the disease for a couple of years, but that he was still living.

"Then it started hitting me—this is the real deal," Krenk said.

So real that doctors had talked to Krenk's mother, who was already on a plane from Washington, where she'd moved with Krenk's stepfather and younger brother. When she arrived, she and Krenk would head to the Mayo Clinic in Rochester, Minnesota.

"I remember I walked out of there, I was crying like a baby, man. I thought I was done," Krenk said. "I mean, I'm going to Mayo Clinic?"

The Spring Game was the next day, and Krenk watched from the sidelines before heading to Minnesota. There he would have another surgery to take more of his middle toe, down to the joint. The doctor warned him, though, that they if they found any further cancer, they would take what they needed to take. If they needed to take his foot, they'd take his foot. If they needed to take his leg, they'd take his leg.

"I remember waking up from surgery and he said, 'We took the rest of that toe, but we didn't find anything,'" Krenk said.

"He goes, 'We can't find cancer anywhere. This is a very strange situation because we've never had someone get Ewing Sarcoma in an area like that and not have cancer somewhere else.'"

An oncologist still suggested chemotherapy, although Krenk, after being advised of possible long-term effects, decided against it. For the next year or two, Krenk returned to the Mayo Clinic every three months for a full battery of tests, then every six months, then once a year. With no re-occurrences, Krenk eventually was able to cease the visits.

The cancer scare and loss of his middle toe didn't sidetrack Krenk's football career. In addition to contributing with the memorable "Bouncerooski" his senior season, Krenk participated in NFL training camps with the Seattle Seahawks and Dallas Cowboys before finally latching on with the Chicago Bears and playing part of the 1984 season. He earned a Super Bowl ring with the Bears in 1985 despite spending much of the season on injured reserve.

In between stints with the Seahawks and Cowboys, Krenk returned to Lincoln in 1983 and received his degree while working as an under-graduate assistant football coach. Krenk was working out on campus one day when Osborne approached him about having not yet graduated and offered Krenk the position while he finished up his coursework.

It all happened because Krenk caught a pass that wasn't really designed for him in the first place.

Had he not caught that pass in place of Williams against Oklahoma State?

"We wouldn't be talking today," Krenk said bluntly. "I swear. We just wouldn't."

—Brian Rosenthal

CHAPTER 10

SCOTT RARIDON

Offensive Tackle, 1979–83

Even the best laid schemes of mice, men, and Hall of Fame offensive line coaches go awry.

Legendary Husker offensive line coach Milt Tenopir was beaming at a Huskers practice in 1983 with his finely tuned O-line on a sunny day with NFL scouts in attendance. Also adding to the pride was the fact that Nebraska was an innovator of a running play that would soon take hold in the NFL—the counter trey.

The counter trey is designed for the offense to fake rushing one way, then attack the defense in the other direction. To be successful, a pulling guard and tackle would need to have great quickness because the linemen need to circle around the field.

Huskers lineman Scott Raridon, from Mason City, Iowa, would be the pulling tackle on the upcoming play. The other pulling lineman was a Midwestern boy too—guard Dean Steinkuhler from Burr, Nebraska.

"Milt is telling the NFL scouts, 'Watch this play, watch this play,' and he just had this big smile on his face," Raridon said.

Aside from the offensive line studs, Tenopir had other players to make him confident on the play. He had a Heisman winner-to-be in Mike Rozier dotting the I-formation with Turner Gill under center, one of the best quarterbacks to ever play at Nebraska.

"On the counter trey I would always tell Dean, 'I'm gonna catch you,' so we would just mess around and have fun with it," Raridon said. "So the play starts and we are both going too fast and we run into each other and trip and we end up on our backs. We just killed the play.

"And I looked up from the ground and see Milt just shaking his head and some scouts looking around like they didn't see the play."

The counter trey would recover as the Washington Redskins would make it a staple of their successful offense on Sundays with Redskins offensive linemen like Joe Jacoby leading the way for bruising running back John Riggins. Raridon would also recover from the comical mishap to become an All-Big 8 selection in 1983.

Coming out of Mason City High School with a decorated prep career, Raridon would go on to be a standout performer who could have picked any school to play at for his college days. However, having a former Husker as his high school coach in Barry Alvarez probably gave Nebraska the inside track to signing the player.

The home-state schools, Iowa and Iowa State, recruited him hard, but the pull to Nebraska was too strong for both Raridon and another soon-to-be Husker from Iowa.

"Me and Roger Craig were the two big recruits out of Iowa and we both went to Nebraska," Raridon said. "I know some folks were not happy in Iowa. But I had a great relationship with Coach [John] Melton and my parents loved Coach Osborne!"

The jovial Melton would bring up Nebraska's rich history and recent success in a humorous way, but it got the point across, especially with Iowa's poor football program for most of the 1960s and 1970s.

"Coach Melton would have on one of those big fancy bowl rings," Raridon said. "And he would flash it to you with a big smile on his face and would say, 'You want one of these? Come to Nebraska!'"

The major bowls helped in Raridon's recruitment, but Osborne was the closer for the big offensive tackle from Iowa. Raridon was impressed with Osborne's style of coaching then and now. During his Huskers career, the coach's ability to communicate the nuts and bolts of the playbook helped the offensive lineman see the big picture while doing his assignment.

"It was no surprise he was an offensive genius," Raridon said. "He clearly explained why we are doing something in this situation or what it was supposed to accomplish. He took the time to show you the whole picture. That was his style of coaching."

Another aspect about Osborne's style stood out to Raridon: Osborne's ability to communicate the nuances of the playbook almost made Raridon able to teach it himself.

"I knew all of the pieces on the play," Raridon said. "Where the I-back would be when I was here, or what I was supposed to achieve. All the pieces fit together and it would make you more focused on your assignment as you knew exactly what you needed to do to make the play a success."

Helping Raridon complete his assignments in his career was a physical attribute not always found in offensive lineman of his size, according to Tenopir.

"For a big guy, Scott had good balance and as a tackle that helps," Tenopir said of the 6'5" offensive lineman.

Physical skills or not, Raridon's role early in his career at Nebraska was not satisfying to him. The beginning of a college career at Nebraska for an offensive lineman in the 1980s was not quite the same, as it took time to get on the field.

Patience was not something Raridon had as an underclassman at Nebraska.

"My big struggle was the grind on the front end in college," Raridon said. "You are this highly recruited guy and everybody back home is asking why aren't you playing. I guess I couldn't see the process at Nebraska as a young guy."

Osborne would help him see the situation with some of his trademark wisdom early in Raridon's career as a Cornhusker, even if the offensive lineman was not expecting to hear it.

"Coach Osborne called me into his office one day and said, 'Scott, if you want to transfer, go ahead,'" Raridon said. "And that really sunk in with me and got me back on track.

"After that I had a different outlook at Nebraska."

That aspect of Osborne's style allowed him to develop trust with his players and clear expectations.

"Coach Osborne always knew just what to say to a player in those situations," Raridon said. "And you knew he cared more than any guy on the planet about you as a person."

Raridon was probably not the first player with whom Osborne had to have a heart-to-heart, or tough-love talk; as he saw it, it was in both parties' best interest for an attitude adjustment.

Besides a better attitude, the process at Nebraska, especially for offensive linemen, was different in 1980 than it is today. Freshmen O-linemen would play on the freshman football team and then redshirt in their second year. It would not be until their third year of college that they got on the varsity field, and maybe then the questions from back home might stop.

Raridon went forward with his redshirt year as a sophomore knowing patience was part of the process. It was a process Raridon was beginning to see clearly and understand its purpose.

"I began to realize the offensive line was a system at Nebraska," Raridon said "where the older guys brought the younger guys along."

The other half of that offensive system was the skill players. Raridon saw some of the best ever to play their positions at Nebraska, as well as a couple of guys who would become College Football Hall of Famers and have productive NFL careers.

"Mike Rozier was just a player who knew when game time was," Raridon said. "Not that he didn't practice hard, but if you tested Mike in the 40, he might have timed at like a 4.7 or 4.6, but in games Mike never got caught from behind."

Another East Coast guy would star on the offense for Nebraska. This wide receiver played like an offensive lineman and Raridon and his buddies appreciated that.

"Irving Fryar was just an incredible athlete. A complete football player," Raridon said. "No shock he went first in the draft. You could wake him up at 3:00 AM and he would run a 4.3.

"And what we really respected about him was that he was a tenacious blocker. We just saw the effort for a wide receiver, and that was probably before Nebraska had such an emphasis on receivers blocking too."

Those two players would be pivotal to reversing a losing trend to Oklahoma for a younger Osborne. Nebraska only beat Oklahoma in the 1970s once (1978) while Osborne was the head coach. NU lost to the Sooners in 1980 as well to start the new decade. Raridon noticed the clashes with the Sooners just had a different feel.

"The speed of that game was just noticeably higher, and the tension, too," Raridon said.

In the 1970s, perhaps NU needed more speed to beat OU, or Oklahoma just got some fortunate bounces late in close games that started to become known as Sooner Magic. Either way, in Raridon's varsity years (1981–83) when NU had more speed, they fared much better in the rivalry game.

With "the Triplets," dubbed by coach Barry Switzer, of Rozier, Fryar, and quarterback Gill, NU would be 3–0 versus the Sooners. Also, it would be one of the rare times Osborne showed some emotion after a game.

The 1981 Nebraska-Oklahoma game was also one of the few times Nebraska would be a favorite in the game. That year OU came limping into the home game while NU's star was rising with the Triplets and Craig, the top running back in the Big 8 in 1981. However, Gill was out for the season with an injury.

The stakes were high and it showed on Osborne's face after the game.

"My sophomore year [1981] when Coach Osborne came in the locker room after we beat Oklahoma, you could just see in his face how relieved he was," Raridon said. "And maybe a little misty, but not a tear. Just relief."

Raridon was right to sense the relief as Nebraska had not won in Norman since the Game of the Century, 10 years earlier. While Gill was out, Mark Mauer filled in and did well. Craig and Rozier each had more than 100 yards on the ground and fullback Phil Bates added 75 rushing yards for the game, with Nebraska winning 37–14. Osborne's postgame comment to the *Lincoln Journal Star* editor echoed those feelings of relief.

Scott Raridon's son, John, plans to play for Mike Riley (left), shown here talking with Huskers All-American quarterback Steve Taylor at the coach's introductory press conference in December 2014. *(Shelby Tilts of Shelby Suzanne Photography)*

"I've taken so much guff over this game, I'm just pleased to win it," Osborne said right after the game. "Even though we had already won the conference title, it would have been a winter of discontent if we hadn't beaten Oklahoma."

Also draining Osborne that day might have been the culmination of a topsy-turvy year. Nebraska lost two of its first three games in 1981 but rebounded to win eight straight games, including the relatively easy win over Oklahoma. The Huskers would face top-ranked Clemson in the Orange Bowl and the way fortunes played out, NU had a shot at a national championship versus the Tigers. However, Nebraska lost to Clemson 22–15 and Osborne's first national title would have to wait.

In 1981, Raridon started to see varsity action and aiding his development at NU was not just Tenopir, but another offensive line coach in Cletus Fischer. The two coaches complimented each other well and had varying degrees of experience in coaching.

Tenopir had been with Nebraska since 1974 and was a high school coach prior. Fischer had been at NU since 1959 on coach Bill Jennings' staff after coaching high school football in Texas and Nebraska. Fischer was also a letterman at NU from 1945 to 1948.

Tenopir was not a coach to get in a player's face, but that did not mean his players gave any less effort according to Raridon.

"Milt was a not a yeller or screamer," Raridon said, "but you played hard for him because you did not want to let him down."

Fischer was able to keep practice light and from time to time gave the players a lasting memory.

In the early 1980s, on Fridays, Nebraska used a down-and-distance drill in which they ran plays with no defense. The offense would run plays to the goal line and then head back to midfield. It became a bit of a race between the O-lineman and Fischer to get back to the 50-yard line.

And the former Husker wanted to beat the current players for fun.

"It got to the point that Cletus and the lineman would start running back to the 50 just before the I-back got over the goal line into the end zone," Raridon said.

One day the mundane drill provided a highlight for the ages.

"So this one practice we run it as usual and all of us are cheating to get back to midfield," Raridon said. "Maybe halfway there, Cletus pulls a hammy and he just pops straight up and grabs his leg but on his one leg he keeps running and hobbling, trying to be the first one to the 50. It was a sight to see.

"It might have been the most re-watched practice clip ever. The film might have gotten worn out we watched Cletus hobbling so many times, but it was gold."

But Fischer would keep the players on their toes in film sessions and the joke was not always on him.

"In film Cletus would call out one of your good blocks and you would get a little pumped up," Raridon said, "but then he would call you by the wrong name.

"It was not until your junior year you realized he was just messing with you."

In 1981 Nebraska was 9–3 and its three losses came by seven points or less, making enthusiasm high for 1982, especially with the returning offensive skills players along with Outland Trophy-winner Dave Rimington.

In Raridon's senior year, NU would be coming off two near misses to be national champions. One of those misses was caused by the opening day opponent in 1983 thanks to a new annual game, the Kickoff Classic, to be played in East Rutherford, New Jersey, at Giants Stadium.

Penn State was the defending national champion and probably not as talented as their championship team the previous year, but according to Raridon, the Huskers had a task to complete versus PSU.

"Revenge was on our mind that day," Raridon said. "It would not have mattered who they had out there. We were going to smoke them."

Smoke them they did by the score of 44–6, and another run at a national championship was off and running. NU cruised through the rest of the non-conference schedule and was rarely challenged in Big 8 play.

NU's perfect record of 12–0 set up a date with Miami in the Orange Bowl for the national championship, and the Hurricanes won in heart-breaking fashion, 81–30.

Right after the Miami game, Raridon was off with the Triplets to play in an All-Star game in San Francisco. Still stinging from the Miami loss, he found some kinship with a rival.

"After the Orange Bowl, I played in the East-West Shrine game and Barry Switzer was our coach," Raridon said. "And he was genuinely upset that we lost that game. Maybe his friendship with Osborne factored in, but he was sad for us."

A few months after the Shrine Bowl, Raridon would get drafted in the 1984 NFL Draft in the sixth round by the Philadelphia Eagles. After his pro experience, Raridon got back into the college game at another national powerhouse.

He started working at Notre Dame in 1986 in their strength and conditioning program. The next year he took over the Fighting Irish strength and conditioning program for two years. In his last year, Notre Dame won the national championship.

The Raridon name has continued to be heard in college football ranks since his playing days thanks to his sons and soon to be again at Nebraska. Raridon's oldest son, Scott Sr., played at Notre Dame, another son, Sam, had a successful high school career but chose not to play in college. His youngest son, John, is in high school and is committed play at Nebraska for coach Mike Riley.

Away from the field, the All-Big 8 player has stood out in business as well. In 1996 he founded Raridon & Associates with Johnson & Johnson as a partner. Raridon & Associates is a medical device distribution company that focuses on orthopedics.

Raridon & Associates is a national leader in a lucrative field and has offices located in five states: Iowa, Nebraska, Missouri, Kansas, and Illinois. The business has five companies under its management and employs close to 90 sales representatives.

Raridon is the boss now, but one of his offensive line coaches said Raridon knew how to be a model employee, so to speak.

"Scott did his job and took his pail to work every day for us," Tenopir said. "He did a good job of anchoring the right side our line."

—Jimmy Sheil

CHAPTER 11

MIKE ROZIER

Running Back, 1981–83

The words of his one-time running backs coach, Mike Corgan, popped into the head of Mike Rozier when only a couple of yards separated the Nebraska running back from the goal line and a UCLA defender who was in his face.

Corgan, who had coached Rozier's position the previous two seasons, was rather strict and to the point. A military guy, Corgan served in the Navy in World War II. He was intimidating. Players would be wise to listen to his every word and pay heed.

So naturally, Rozier remembered what Corgan once told him.

"He said, 'You get that close to the goal line, you better score, or we're going to give it to somebody else,'" Rozier said. "So naturally, I wanted to score."

Rozier did, although not in the way many had expected.

Nebraska had the ball at the 2-yard line that September game in 1983. Offensive tackle Scott Raridon pulled and ran to the left to provide a lead block for Rozier on a pitch play. Rozier loved pitch plays. His favorite: "28 pitch."

Rozier took the ball and began running to his left. Then he changed his mind.

"I just saw mostly UCLA players on my left," Rozier said. "I said, 'Then reverse your field. They're ain't nobody on this side.' I had a little speed. I don't think you could really catch me going back against the grain."

He was right. They couldn't. Not even Don Rogers, one of UCLA's top defensive backs who later played for the Cleveland Browns. Rozier said Rogers, who died of a cocaine overdose at age 23, was one of the best players he faced.

"Me and him used to battle all the time," Rozier said, referring to their encounters in the NFL, too. "He ran to one side, [and] tried to catch me."

But Rogers couldn't. Nobody from UCLA could. Rozier, making a big loop to the right side, snuck inside the right pylon for one of the

Mike Rozier will live forever at Memorial Stadium alongside fellow Heisman winners Johnny Rodgers and Eric Crouch. *(Shelby Tilts of Shelby Suzanne Photography)*

longest two-yard touchdown runs you'll ever see. Rozier has heard so many different figures of the amount of yards he actually covered on that play that he's not sure which is correct or what to believe. Some have calculated it to be around 80 yards, maybe more. All for two yards, officially. Oh, and a touchdown in Nebraska's 42–10 victory at Memorial Stadium.

"I've had so many different yardages told to me," Rozier said. "I just know that I scored, and we won."

To this day, that play makes highlight videos. People make a big deal about it. Rozier isn't sure why. It's not that big of a play to him, even if it's considered one of the signature moments of his 1983 Heisman Trophy season.

"That was all natural to me. It wasn't a big thing, but everybody makes it a big thing. I wanted to score," Rozier said. "It was just natural to me. I'd done it several times before. It was no big thing to me."

That Corgan's words stuck in Rozier's head that day should come as no surprise. Rozier, who rushed for a school-record 2,148 yards that season, and ran for a school-record 4,780 yards in his three-year Nebraska career, credits the demanding, no-nonsense coaching approach of Corgan, who served as Rozier's position coach in 1981 and 1982 before Frank Solich took over coaching the running backs in 1983.

"He was a military guy, and we'd always have contact every day in practice, me and Roger [Craig] and the line," Rozier said of Corgan, "and we'd beat each other up—not real bad, but as far as contact, as far as practice."

Rozier remembers going one-on-one with the linebackers, "and I used to hate that," he said.

"When I'd run the ball, my style of running, Mike always told me to put my arms down. He'd call it the lift drill," Rozier said. "I actually used to lift people off me when I ran the ball. I got that from Mike. He kept on practicing with me, and he instilled that in me."

Here's the essence of the lift drill; Rozier would run through a line of six or eight guys—not tackling dummies, mind you, but actual players—as coaches made good use of the extra numbers because of the many walk-ons within the program.

"It was just a line you had to go through," Rozier said. "Instead of having bags, it was live people. You run through, and then they hit on you. I used to hate that. I had to get people off me. If you saw my style of running, I actually threw my forearm at people and would knock them off me. That was the drill, to get them off me.

"Instead of running out of bounds or trying to make a move, I started noticing if you give the guy more contact, they don't really want to tackle you. They'd be scared of you. Then you could start juking them or make a move somewhere else."

Rozier, a native of Camden, New Jersey, could've played football at Penn State. Or Rutgers. Or Pittsburgh. Or any number of schools in the eastern United States, all of which was much closer to home than Lincoln, Nebraska. But that's precisely why Rozier headed to the Midwest. He wanted to get away from home, away from New Jersey, and grow up on his own, away from the shadow of his parents and family, even though they had an extremely close bond.

"College was the best time of my life," Rozier said. "I think college should be the best time of any kid's life. I had a great time, man. You're young, you're experiencing different things, and you're away from home. You learn how to grow up faster."

Nebraska, meanwhile, hadn't really been aware of Rozier until coaches noticed this high school running back playing for the opposing team while studying film of a player they really were recruiting—Billy Griggs, a tight end from Pennsauken High School who eventually played at the University of Virginia and later was drafted by the New York Jets.

"They were looking at Billy, and I was playing against Billy, and they had seen me on film, and that's how they came over to my school," said Rozier, who played for Woodrow Wilson High School, a main rival of Pennsauken. "They really were looking at Billy Griggs. It just so happened my school was playing against Pennsauken at the time."

The coach in charge of convincing Rozier to choose Nebraska? Solich, the longtime assistant who eventually succeeded legendary Tom Osborne as head coach.

"I called him Frankie G, because he always dressed like GQ all the time," Rozier said. "To this day, I still call him Frankie G. He was like my father. Coach [Tom] Osborne was like my father, too. Those guys, I could talk to them, any problems, stuff like that. Their families, I could remember his kids being little when he came down to recruit me.

"Coach Osborne never cussed. I can say that. His cuss word was 'Dagummit.' When Coach Osborne said that, I knew he was mad. Everybody knew he was mad. That was his cuss word."

To this day, Rozier phones Solich's wife, Pam, every Mother's Day. He calls Solich on every Father's Day.

Rozier said he had a "decent" high school football career. Decent enough that many of the college heavyweights began coming after him during his senior season. They began backing off, though, when they took notice of his low grade-point average.

Nebraska, of course, hung on. Osborne wanted Rozier to go to Coffeyville Junior College in Coffeyville, Kansas, where he needed to attend only one year of school, at that time, to become academically eligible at Nebraska.

"I took a Greyhound bus all the way down from Jersey to Coffeyville, because my parents couldn't afford to fly me nowhere, and I cried all the way down," Rozier said. "That was the beginning of my life away from home, in a little small town, Coffeyville. Nice people. Good fans, good football program, good coach. Dick Foster was my coach."

Coffeyville won all nine of its games that 1980 season, and Rozier ran for 1,157 yards, averaging 7.4 yards per carry.

"Every day," he said, "I was getting ready for the University of Nebraska."

When Rozier officially visited Lincoln for the first time, Jarvis Redwine and I.M. Hipp were the Husker I-backs, and fullback Andra Franklin was responsible for showing Rozier around campus and Lincoln.

"It was cold as hell in Nebraska," Rozier said of that visit. "The University was real big. Everything was red and white. I had a good visit, they took me around the weight room, had Valentino's pizza, meeting people. I just remember it was cold. I'll never forget that.

"I was surrounded by a bunch of good people. My mom and dad were positive, keeping me in school. There were a couple of times I wanted to quit, but they kept me in, talked to me. Coach Osborne talked to me. Frank Solich talked to me. I was just homesick. A kid from Jersey coming to Nebraska, my first time away from home—we're a real close-knit family, and that was the first time I was away from home."

Wingback Irving Fryar, another New Jersey native and part of the same high school recruiting class as Rozier, had already played a season with the Huskers by the time Rozier arrived from junior college. Rozier said the two had decided together they would attend Nebraska, even though junior college delayed Rozier's arrival by one season.

Fryar, quarterback Nate Mason, split end Ricky Simmons, and running back Roger Craig were among the players Rozier would hang out with most, both on and off the field. Fryar and Rozier joined quarterback Turner Gill as the famous "Triplets" in the 1983 Scoring Explosion offense, considered the greatest offensive team in Nebraska history.

Combine those skills players with a star-studded offensive line, and perhaps it's not entirely shocking to hear Rozier claim he wasn't even the best player on his team, let alone the nation, when he won the Heisman Trophy in a landside. (Rozier, by the way, said he had no nerves the night of that award presentation in New York. "In my mind," he said, "I had a good feeling I'd won it.")

"My offensive line was great—Dean Steinkuhler, Dave Rimington—some guys in the first round [of the NFL Draft]. Just because I won the Heisman, I wouldn't say I was the best player. If it wasn't for those guys blocking for me and doing things downfield, I never would've won the Heisman.

"My linemen blocked good. I used to tell them, 'Just give me an inch, just give me a little hole, I can get through that.' I had great blockers, as far as linemen, and my receivers. I think that helped out for me a whole a lot, because my receivers blocked for me downfield."

What's more, Rozier remembers Nebraska's talent up and down the depth chart, not just on the first team. The second team was just as good, in his eyes.

"We didn't miss a beat when I came out and Jeff [Smith] came in, or Irv went out and Ricky Simmons came in. Anybody could've been a starter if they had left Nebraska to play somewhere else."

The upperclassmen on the 1981 team had little idea who Rozier was—until the Spring Game that year, when they quickly learned about the transfer from Coffeyville. Guys like Sammy Sims and Russell Gary and others expressed their surprise, Rozier recalls.

"Just a bunch of guys were like, 'Who is this guy? He's running the ball like he's going crazy.' Everybody knew who I was then," Rozier said. "I was gifted. I was real blessed. My second team offense, they were decent."

Decent enough for Rozier to run the ball on the number one defense to the tune of 180 yards in the Spring Game.

He impressed his sophomore season with a 93-yard touchdown run against Kansas State, the first of many memorable plays and performances in his illustrious career. A couple of games stick out to Rozier, though, both of which involved injury.

To Rozier, that dazzling run against UCLA pales in comparison to his gutsy performance against Missouri in 1982, when he played the second half with a painful hip-pointer, playing only because Nebraska was trailing at halftime.

"I went in, and I got a shot. They shot me up," Rozier said. "I'm not even sure how you get hip-pointers. I'd never had one, but if you ask anyone who's ever had one, it hurts real bad. You can't laugh. You can't go to the bathroom. I mean, it hurts."

Still, Rozier rushed for 66 yards in a 79-yard game-winning touchdown drive in Nebraska's 23–19 victory over the Tigers. He finished with 139 rushing yards in a performance trainer George Sullivan said matched anything he'd seen in his 31 years at Nebraska.

"If that had been Herschel Walker or anybody else, he would have been on the sidelines getting publicity," Rimington, the team captain and 1981 Outland Trophy winner, told reporters after the game. "Not Mike Rozier. He just went in hurt and still got 139 yards."

Sullivan told the *Lincoln Journal Star* after the game, "After we got that last touchdown, Rozier came over to me, asked for the icepack and said, 'I can't pick it up no more.'

In Rozier's final collegiate performance, the famous 1984 Orange Bowl game against Miami, he ran for 125 yards in the first half. Those were his final yards as a Husker. A severe ankle sprain before halftime kept him from returning.

"We were going down to score, it was '28-pitch,' right side, and a little defensive back guy, I think it was number five, little short guy, he got me down by my ankles," Rozier said. "Once he hit me, I tried to get up on it. I couldn't get on it. I even went inside and got it shot up and everything. I still couldn't do nothing. I tried. I definitely wanted to win."

Without Rozier and chasing an undefeated season and national championship, Nebraska still rallied against Miami on its home field. His backup, Jeff Smith, scored on a fourth-down option run to the right in the final minute, setting up one of the most famous play calls in sports history—Osborne's decision, down 31–30, to go for the two-point conversion.

Rozier was on the sideline when the call was made.

"Coach Osborne asked everybody. He didn't just make the call on his own," Rozier said. "We were beating everybody up that year, so we could've won it by tying it up—we could've won the national championship. But we wanted to go out as a winner, so we decided to go for it."

In Rozier's mind, the failed attempt—Gill's pass was batted away in the end zone—wasn't the sole reason Nebraska's run at perfection fell short.

"I still think if I don't get hurt—I'm not saying I'm all that—but I know for a fact if I didn't get hurt and I played the third and fourth quarters, we would've won that game," Rozier said. "No doubt.

"It's funny how people still talk about that game," Rozier said, recalling the number of times he's seen the game on ESPN Classic. "The guys still talk about that game. They still talk about that team. I was part of that team, so it makes me feel proud."

Also memorable for Rozier were his three times playing in the famed Nebraska-Oklahoma rivalry. Even in high school and growing up on the East Coast, Rozier could remember the significance of the annual Thanksgiving-time game.

"And now I'm in that big game," Rozier said. "Everybody's watching me, watching my teammates. I always wanted to do the best job I could while I was out there. The players we had on my team, we were real confident. We had some good ball players. Not just me. My line was great, my defense was great. We were like a little family.

"I can remember every time we played Oklahoma, Coach Osborne would always get a little tight—I called it tight booty—during that week of practice. Everything had to be just perfect. You had to be on time. But we always just looked around like, 'We're going to beat 'em. We're going to come to practice and do the things we're capable of doing.'"

And they did. Rozier won all three times he played Oklahoma, part of a rare winning streak for Osborne against coaching rival Barry Switzer.

But the biggest memory Rozier has of his time at Nebraska?

"They had great fans. I'm serious," he said. "I don't care where I go, to this day, I still talk about the fans. They always support us. Wherever we go, they're always there for us. It reminds me a little bit of Green Bay. Nebraska is similar like that. It's like a little family thing there."

—Brian Rosenthal

CHAPTER 12

JERRY MURTAUGH, JUNIOR YEAR

1969

Before the 1969 season Coach Melton finally accepted the situation with Murtaugh, but he did have a request of the rambunctious linebacker to make the situation livable.

"Just stay away from Coach Devaney," Melton said. "He doesn't even want to look at you."

Murtaugh said he complied with it, even if it created an odd relationship for an important player and head coach.

"I did that the best I could," Murtaugh said. "After my freshman year I think in four years he never talked to me, he just yelled at me. Nothing was ever said if I played well after a game...maybe once he congratulated me after a game. And that was fine. If I played bad, just tell me."

In 1969 the Huskers and the coach put some unrest to bed with a bounce-back season by going 9–2 after back-to-back 6–4 seasons in 1967 and 1968. The unrest was such that a petition was circulated in the state to fire the NU staff. Legend has it some assistant coaches signed the petition.

Murtaugh was a big reason the petition never gained too much steam. He was a defensive standout in 1969 and led the team in tackles with 111. Also, he tacked on two interceptions to show he could do more than drop a ballcarrier and upset Devaney.

NU put an exclamation point on the regular season by pummeling Oklahoma of 44–14. The game was a form of revenge for Murtaugh personally after the Sooners had their way with the Huskers in 1968. Leading the attack for the Sooners was running back Steve Owens. On the day, he rushed for five touchdowns and 172 yards, plus he had a little something extra for Murtaugh.

"They whupped us like 600 to nothing," said Murtaugh of the 47–0 score. "Every time after a tackle, Steve would end on top of me as they were killing us and he would say, 'Hey! How is your day going, Murtaugh?'

"And I didn't say anything back. It was maybe the only time I kept my mouth shut. What could I say?"

Murtaugh finished the game with maybe 20 tackles, and this was a rare occasion on which Devaney broke his "silence" to Murtaugh. After the game Devaney yelled at everyone else about the blowout loss, but he told the Omaha native in a normal voice, "Good game, Murtaugh."

Murtaugh remembered Owens the following year when Nebraska took Oklahoma behind the woodshed 44–14.

"Every time I hit Steve Owens, I was on top of him this time," Murtaugh said. "And I said, 'How ya doing Stevie? Having a good day?'

"This time, Stevie said nothing," Murtaugh said.

Beating Oklahoma usually meant being Big 8 champions and heading to Miami, but in 1969 that was not that case as Missouri won the conference. Nebraska headed to the Sun Bowl in the border town of El Paso, Texas… across the river from Juarez, Mexico.

With a few days to kill before the game in El Paso, Murtaugh had an idea. His thought was to get the boys together and head to Juarez in the afternoon.

What could go wrong on a sunny afternoon in Mexico with offensive linemen Wally Winter and Bob "Fig" Newton, running back Jeff Hughes, and defensive linemen Denny Gutzman and Eddie Periard?

"It was a Tuesday or Wednesday during the day and everybody went over to Juarez," Murtaugh said. "We go to this place and we are having a great time just drinking, tequila probably. And there was this band that was gonna play later on but there was nobody on stage yet, and there were no signs that said 'Stay off the stage.'

"So Jeff jumped up on stage and started playing the drums, somebody else jumps up and starts singing. We were just being clowns and dancing on stage."

They got down from the stage with no harm done and they did a few shots. Shortly after, Murtaugh went outside to get some air.

Soon enough he wasn't the only person outside.

"It was around 5:00-ish in the afternoon and I go outside for some reason," Murtaugh said, "and then all of a sudden I have never seen so many cop cars show up at once…and I'm used to cop cars showing up!

"And all these little Mexican police officers pile out of the cars with their guns pulled and rush into the bar."

But one of the gun-drawn cops had a sixth sense about Murtaugh and went straight to him to make sure the linebacker would not be going back into the bar.

"And then this midget police officer comes up to me and sticks this big gun in my belly button," Murtaugh said, "and he is looking up at me speaking all Spanish. I have no idea what he is saying or what is going on; all I know is I have a little guy with a gun on me."

It might have only been five minutes but it seemed like an hour Murtaugh said before there was any resolution.

"So finally they bring out Wally, Denny, Eddie, and Hughes. They put them in cars and take off," Murtaugh said. "I'm screaming…and I'm looking for Fig (Bob Newton), but I found out later Fig ran out the back door when it started going down. Just like an offensive player to bug out!"

When reached for comment Newton said, "I wasn't sticking around when the cops barged in. I somehow got back across the border by myself to the hotel, too."

Murtaugh knew he had to get them out of jail as quick as possible to avoid the wrath of Devaney.

"I sat there for a little bit and figured I needed two things," Murtaugh said. "I got to find where the police station is and I got to get bail money for the guys."

Murt accomplished those goals after about an hour of wandering around Juarez and El Paso. However, he forgot to take some souvenirs out of his pockets when he went to the police station.

"I found the station, which is where they had a little court too. Then I found an interpreter," Murtaugh said. "The judge comes in and the

(L to R) Bob Newton, Jeff Hughes, Jerry Murtaugh, and Wally Winter just hours before getting arrested in Juarez, Mexico, and incurring the wrath of Bob Devaney. *(Courtesy of Jerry Murtaugh)*

judge speaks whatever he does and then a cop comes up and frisks me and I thought, 'Oh shit,' because I forgot I had four switchblades on me. Real nice ones, too, with pearl handles that I bought in Juarez."

Murtaugh figured he might be in the cell next to his buddies as he put the concealed weapons on the bench with the money.

"I put the wad of money and the switchblades on the bench and the judge just looks at me like he can't believe how dumb I am," Murtaugh said. "The interpreter told me the judge said he will let them go, but he said don't you ever come over to Juarez again.

"Then they marched the jailbirds out and we left."

But Murtaugh wanted his switchblades.

"I started to turn around to leave and then I remembered I forgot my switchblades," Murtaugh said, "and I reached up and that gavel came down right next to my hand almost between my fingers and the judge is hollering something. The interpreter says something dirty to me in Spanish and then he said, 'You better get out of here before you get arrested!'"

The players got on a bus and headed back to the team hotel. It was no surprise to Murtaugh who was waiting for the bus at the team hotel.

"So we get on a bus and when we get back to the hotel there is Devaney with steam coming out of his little head," Murtaugh said. "You can see his little head was red."

Murtaugh did not avoid the wrath of the head coach.

"Whoever got off first he yelled at, whoever got off second he yelled at," Murtaugh said. "Then I get off and he pulled me to the side and he called me filthy names and you did it, you got them arrested, blah, blah...."

"And I'm yelling back at Devaney that I didn't get arrested and that I actually got them out of jail."

Devaney was not buying it, even if this was one of the few times Murtaugh was not the one who got arrested. The coach decided to make an example out of them. He kicked them all off the team and said they would be flying home the next day.

The players huddled up to ponder if Devaney was serious and what might happen to their lives if so. Some talked about their possible pro careers and some mentioned the trouble they would be in at home if Devaney followed through on his threat.

But, as usual, Murtaugh had a couple of answers.

"I said, 'If I got kicked off the team, I wouldn't be in much trouble; my dad would say he was surprised I got this far.'"

Then Murtaugh laid it out to them why they should not be scared.

"Devaney is not going to kick us off the team, calm down, we are starters, he needs us," Murtaugh said. "But he will get us after the game in Lincoln."

The gathering broke up and they went to bed. Soon Devaney was doing personal bed-checks with some assistant coaches. Murtaugh could hear Devaney yelling as they went from room to room. The linebacker was not going to make it easy on the head coach when Devaney came to his room.

"I get a knock on my door and I just yelled 'What?' in sorta an irritated tone," Murtaugh said.

That was not the answer Devaney wanted to hear and he burst into the room and started yelling at Murtaugh as basically the ringleader of all the trouble. Some inappropriate language was used by both player and coach as they picked up where they left off earlier in the parking lot for round two of the verbal battle.

"I yelled back something nasty at him," Murtaugh said, "but I was just lying in bed real calm-like because I knew he was not gonna get rid of me because he needs me to win and I am a starter."

Finally Murtaugh's nonchalance was too much for the coach, who was used to having total control of his program, and Devaney upped the ante.

"But then Devaney said he was going to beat the shit out of me," Murtaugh said. "And I jumped out of that bed and said, 'Come on old man, I will kick your ass!'

"He came at me but the coaches grabbed this little man and the coaches are holding him back and his little feet are flopping in the air because he wanted me bad."

The assistant coaches were trying to control the situation but Murtaugh was not making their job any easier.

"And I'm yelling, 'Let him go, let him go,' and they are yelling at me to shut up," Murtaugh said. "They are telling Devaney to get out of there before something happens.

"And I said, 'Yeah, I'm gonna kick his ass!' The coaches are going nuts, and Melton is about to have a heart attack."

Finally sanity was restored with no punches being thrown in Murtaugh's hotel room, and the coaches left. The nightcap was a phone call to each of the offending players from an assistant coach. They were told they had a meeting in the morning with Devaney and they had better be there on time.

"So we go to this meeting and Devaney starts in on us," Murtaugh said. "He says, 'I oughta kick you off the team but I will handle this when we get back to Lincoln!'

"Once I heard 'I oughta' I had to look down to keep from laughing. I think he was staring at me too, just looking for an excuse to yell at me. And at the end of the meeting he says to us, 'And you better have a good game!'"

They did have a good game, beating Georgia soundly 42–6. But the highlight of the trip, for Murtaugh anyway, might have been watching Devaney and his wife discuss their mutual acquaintance.

"My wife had just shown up the day before the game," Murtaugh said. "And we are going down to lunch or something and he grabbed my wife and pulled her to the side. He said, 'You have to control him! You have to keep him out of jail, we just can't have this.'

"I heard my wife say, 'Well…how am I supposed to do that?'

And Devaney yelled, "You are his wife!"

When the team returned to Lincoln, Newton said Devaney did indeed take action against the offending players.

He took their free movie theater passes away.

—*Jimmy Sheil*

CHAPTER 13

HARRY GRIMMINGER
Offensive Lineman, 1980–84

By 1983, Nebraska had established itself as one the most physical rushing teams in the country, with bruising offensive linemen that had the hardware to prove it. Husker offensive linemen had won back-to-back Outland Trophies, had a three-year streak of All-Americans, and a six-year streak of two or more offensive linemen on the All-Big 8 team (1977–82).

Nebraska featured the kind of linemen who would pancake your mom if that's what it took to move the sticks. On his way to his first start as a Cornhusker., Harry Grimminger didn't exactly look like a mother-flattening offensive lineman that most teams would fear.

"On the bus to the Penn State game in my Walkman I was listening to polka by Frankie Yankovic," Grimminger said. "I'm not sure on the song, maybe 'Happy Mountaineer' by Frankie."

Whether or not America's King of Polka helped Grimminger that day is unknown, as it was not in legendary NU Sports Information Director Don Bryant's postgame notes. However, Grimminger and Nebraska had their way with the Nittany Lions, winning 44–6 in the Kickoff Classic to start the 1983 season.

While his music tastes were unique for a football player, his recruitment was standard; maybe all too common for a Cornhusker state player.

"I wasn't in demand coming out of high school, and just like any Nebraska kid I wanted to play in Lincoln," the 6'3", 270-pound offensive guard said. "I was a low-talent, high-effort type of guy."

His position coach at Nebraska somewhat agreed with Grimminger's review of himself. The hall of fame college coach said Grimminger helped the successful process of Husker offensive linemen continue as well.

"Harry came to us from Grand Island and he was a hard worker," Tenopir, who coached at Nebraska from 1974 to 2002, said. "Harry was an overachiever but he did have some ability, as he was an All-American in his last year with us.

"His work ethic stood out, and that was a great thing for the younger guys coming up to see as well."

Grimminger's hard work began on the freshman team in 1980. The freshmen went 5–0 against a schedule of smaller college JVs. Playing with Grimminger on offense was one of coach Tom Osborne's early recruiting wins versus Oklahoma, Turner Gill.

Gill was a highly sought quarterback out of Texas and Barry Switzer wanted him as badly as Osborne desired the signal-caller. Gill showed early why the best coaches in the country wanted him under center on Saturdays.

"Right off the bat you could see Turner was a leader with the way he carried himself," Grimminger said. "He had that look in his eye like he was going places. He was always very composed and determined to get the job done, and you were ready to go with him."

The freshmen team was coached by Frank Solich and Cletus Fischer. Grimminger played for Fischer's brother, Ken, in high school and there was some familiarity from the beginning for the Grand Island product. Fischer coached the offensive lineman on the varsity team with Tenopir and was good-natured and could laugh at himself, according to Grimminger.

"When we used to split up in practice for lineman drills we would run behind Cletus," Grimminger said. "Cletus took these short choppy steps and he ran like a duck. So we would run behind him going quack, quack. He loved that. He could hardly run he was laughing so hard."

Those types of relationships, and characters, were common on head coach Tom Osborne's staff, and not only on the offensive side of the ball. A defensive coach was good for laughs during practice, as well. Charlie McBride had just come to NU in 1977 and took over as defensive coordinator in 1981. His style was not to mince words.

"Charlie used to call Thursdays and Fridays 'Pussies and Fairies Day,'" Grimminger said, "He called it that because we would just be in shorts with no contact, but all the guys who couldn't really play all that well would be going 100 mph and you would be like, 'Where was this all week?'"

However, the coach most responsible for Grimminger's development was Tenopir. His style was rooted in teaching the basics of blocking from his previous experience. Before coming to Nebraska, Tenopir was a high school coach in small towns in Nebraska, Colorado, and Kansas.

"Milt stayed on you and made you consistent with fundamentals," Grimminger said. "We used to work on right step, left step, eight step, left stop, nonstop, all day long."

And when the coaching got a bit more complex, he would be there to keep the players giving effort, even if it wasn't coming easy.

"He never gave up on you. 'You'll get there!' he would say," Grimminger said. "Milt knew how to coach the basics and build on it and motivate you."

Grimminger also noted that his style was based on what he knew was needed for the Husker offense, which he was partially responsible for creating with Tom Osborne.

"Milt knew what we needed to do in our offense with drop step and pulling by the offensive linemen," Grimminger said. "As linemen he drilled into us that we knew we needed 'to clear the trash so there would not be any penetration.'"

But the jargon of practice is only a minor part of what his players remember about Tenopir 30 years later.

"Milt talks at the Omaha Businessman Association routinely and each year there are different Huskers there and he has a story about every guy there," Grimminger said. "He didn't even coach or recruit Ricky Simmons and said 'We got Ricky from Texas' and then told two stories about him. Milt is a real genuine relationship type guy."

Grimminger was just starting to get in Tenopir's pipeline in 1981 with a redshirt year. After freshman ball, as was customary at the time, many linemen would take a redshirt year. It would give them a year to get stronger and more comfortable with the playbook while doing a lot of watching.

Harry Grimminger at Memorial Stadium in 2003 with his nephew, Cooper, for Harry's induction into the Nebraska Football Hall of Fame. *(Courtesy of Harry Grimminger)*

In 1981 the NU varsity team started slow but rebounded to win the Big 8 and was ranked No. 4 in the country at the end of the regular season. Their bowl game would be against the Clemson Tigers, ranked No. 1 in the polls, in the Orange Bowl with a freshman named William 'The Refrigerator" Perry.

As fate would have it, the two teams ahead of NU lost and the night game in the Orange Bowl with Clemson would be for all the marbles. Clemson did win 22–15, but Grimminger had a front-row seat for a physical display by a Husker lineman.

"Rimington beat the hell out of the Fridge in that game," Grimminger said of the future NFL veterans' battle.

In fairness to Perry, he was a freshman and Rimington was a junior, but he still got whipped according to Grimminger.

Grimminger would make an early impact at Nebraska in his first season on the varsity team. He was a backup in 1982 to Dean Steinkuhler at right guard.

"Dean was so such an all-around talent with his speed and power," Grimminger said. "He was just the complete package for an offensive lineman. His overall versatility made him so unique."

Grimminger was two-deep on a team that only lost one game on their way to winning the Big 8 championship and the Orange Bowl in 1982; the one loss was a controversial defeat to Penn State on the road. Penn State rallied late with some unusual calls to pull out the win. Longtime football analyst Beano Cook said a Penn State receiver was on the Schuylkill Expressway when he caught a fourth-down pass to keep the Nittany Lion game-winning drive alive.

However, that game was likely fuel for NU (along with Frankie Yankovic) to start the 1983 season. After the relatively easy Penn State win, Nebraska's next big non-conference game would be with UCLA and it would be memorable for many reasons.

One of the most famous plays in Nebraska football history—and impactful, as it became part of a Heisman campaign—was due in large part to a blown assignment from Grimminger.

As the Huskers lined up near the Bruin goal line early in the second quarter, Osborne called a "49 pitch" to the left on a third-and-goal from the 2-yard line. It was not Grimminger's finest play, but his effort saved any total disgrace.

"I had a poor block on a guy that blew up that play but Mike broke his tackle at the five-yard line and then he reversed field," Grimminger said. "I knew Mike was still going and I could feel the way the play was going so I kept going and you never give up on a play, even if you fouled it up. And I threw a block he really didn't need at the end of the play that I got credit for."

In Husker lore some say Rozier ran 80 yards to get two yards and Grimminger actually did get some credit from a jubilant Lyell Bremser right after the play on the radio.

"This man, Mike Rozier...started running the left side! He was shut off on the left side, far to the left sideline! He turned, reversed his field, came all the way across to the right side...picking up blockers as he came! Came laterally across the field, back at about the 10-yard line, he turned up field when he got a block or two from Turner Gill, his quarterback, and Harry Grimminger, his left guard, among others! And went into the end zone...believe it or not, for the touchdown!"

That type of effort versus UCLA is why Rozier was the type of running back for whom lineman would go all out on plays. Even if they were not perfect, it was usually good enough.

"Mike was the kind of back that made us offensive linemen look good," Grimminger said. "We did not have to be perfect. He would have a way of making defensive guys commit and then bounce outside and he was gone. He was not a dancer but he had some moves. He got north-south quickly."

The Huskers pulled away from UCLA after Rozier's adventurous run and pretty much ran away from most of the teams they played in 1983. Aside from the "Triplets" stars in Gill, Rozier, and wingback Irving Fryar, NU had one of the best O-lines in Husker history with three players who would make the All-Big 8 team in Steinkuhler, Scott Raridon, and Mark Traynowicz in addition to Grimminger, who would make All-American the next season.

The 1983 Husker offense is also recognized as one of the best in college football. NU averaged more than 400 rushing yards a game, becoming one of three teams to do it in college football history. They also scored an average of 52 points a game.

The 1983 Huskers were on pace to not only win the National Championship but to be regarded as one of the all-time great teams. They defeated Oklahoma in the last week of the regular season to set the stage with No. 5 Miami in the Orange Bowl. The Hurricanes would be getting a home game for all intents and purposes.

Nebraska stood atop the polls, and Texas, which was going to the Cotton Bowl, was No. 2. When the Longhorns lost earlier on January 2, it turned the Orange Bowl game into a national championship contest for both teams.

Even if the field was not championship quality.

"I remember getting in my stance and my finger sinking up to my first knuckle into the sand that was painted green," Grimminger said. "There was very little grass since the field was so torn up by the Miami Dolphins by the end of their year."

Grimminger said NU was ready to play but still got off to a slow start versus Miami on the Hurricanes' home-field. Miami raced to a 17–0 lead, but Nebraska battled back to tie the game in the third quarter. Miami built a 14-point second half lead but again, NU stormed back.

Late in the fourth quarter, on fourth-and-8 on a textbook option by Gill to I-back Jeff Smith, who was filling in for an injured Rozier, the

Huskers scored on a 24-yard run to pull within 31–30 with 48 seconds left to play.

Osborne went for the two-point conversion and a possible win, but it was unsuccessful.

Grimminger thought the attempt at the two-point conversion was the right call. You play to win as Osborne did, he said, even if kicking the extra point would have meant a national championship.

"But Miami was just a little better on that play," Grimminger said. Miami defensive back Ken Calhoun had knocked away Gill's pass to the NU tight end.

While the last game of 1983 was disappointing for Grimminger and Nebraska, the Huskers picked up right where they left off in 1984. Early in the season Nebraska was near the top of the polls with another matchup with UCLA. The Bruins were confident going into the game, said Grimminger.

They shouldn't have been.

"We beat them fairly easily the year before but for some reason they were saying things about really taking it to us before the 1984 game in LA," Grimminger said. "And we just went through them again. I mean they were giving up five yards just to make a tackle. Not real tough football players."

Nebraska won 42–3 that day and Grimminger was named Player of the Game by the announcers for his efforts leading the way for running back Smith, who would make the cover of *Sports Illustrated* that week.

Maybe it was the *Sports Illustrated* cover jinx, but the following week Syracuse came ready to hit. The No. 1 ranked Huskers had breezed through the first three weeks, winning easily each Saturday, and had crushed the Orangemen the year before 63–7 in Lincoln. Syracuse was led by head coach Dick MacPherson and they were coming off their first winning season since 1979 in 1984, but the Huskers were still heavy favorites in the matchup in the Carrier Dome.

Grimminger said Osborne and the staff prepared the team for the noise, but it was much greater than expected on that Saturday in upstate New York. NU's offense never got in a rhythm and lost 17–9. After a first-quarter touchdown, Nebraska could not string together many first downs.

Actually, the Huskers had the ball for only 23 minutes, while Syracuse had it for 36-plus. It was role reversal for the Big Red, which had some injury issues as well. NU was without the nation's leading I-back in Smith, but sophomore Doug DuBose played well by rushing for 107 yards on 23 carries. The loss ended a 23-game regular-season winning streak for Nebraska.

Later in the season Nebraska would rebound thanks in large part to the defense as the Blackshirts would end up as one of the top units in the country. At each level they had defensive playmakers.

"Jim Skow was something else," Grimminger said of the defensive lineman. "He wasn't the biggest guy but he was fast. Undersized too but [he] was as tough as a junkyard dog."

The linebackers featured a duo that complemented each other.

"(Mike) Knox was such a tough guy and [Marc] Munford could go sideline to sideline with his speed and make plays," Grimminger said. "Knox could run too, but he was the guy who would step in the hole and smack somebody."

The defensive backs were led by a smooth future All-American.

"Bret Clark was just a good-looking athlete," Grimminger said. "He was close to 6'4" and could run and hit."

Clark ended up a two-time All-Big 8 selection along with All-American honors before a solid four-year pro career that was cut short by injuries. He proved his ability at Nebraska, holding Husker marks for career unassisted tackles by a defensive back, passes broken up in a season, and passes broken up in a career after his senior year.

The 1984 defense got more headlines than they did the previous year, but the offense had all-conference performers who also earned their keep throughout the season. Grimminger along with center Traynowicz and offensive tackle Mark Behning were All Big-8. Also, Grimminger and Traynowicz would make the All-American team.

As NU mounted another national championship charge in 1984, an old foe tripped them up again. Oklahoma would beat Nebraska for first since 1980 by the score of 17–7 in Lincoln. However, Grimminger's career would end on a winning note with a victory over LSU in the Orange Bowl 28–10.

Grimminger signed a free-agent contract with the Seattle Seahawks after his Husker days were over. But soon, he focused on a career in education with his degree. After working in the Grand Island Public School until 2000, he became an assistant principal at Millard West High School in Omaha.

One of his duties at Millard West incudes discipline for freshmen. It is a well-known fact that high school freshmen are some of the most interesting creatures on the earth. If Grimminger might look quizzically at his pupils now and again, one of his coaches looked at him that way too.

"One day at practice Harry showed up wearing a black armband. I asked who died," Tenopir said. "And Harry replied with a smile, like I should have known, that it was country music star Ernie Bell.

"Harry was a good and interesting one alright."

—Jimmy Sheil

CHAPTER 14

MIKE ANDERSON

Linebacker, 1989–93

The Huskers freshman linebacker did not feel like Nebraska pulled a bait-and-switch on him during recruiting, but playing linebacker at Nebraska was not what he expected.

At all.

A change in the linebackers coach from his high school senior year to his first year at Nebraska would alter Mike Anderson's Huskers experience. When Anderson was looking at going to Nebraska out of Grand Island High School in 1988, he was being recruited by longtime Husker assistant coach, the happy-go-lucky John Melton.

On a recruiting visit to Nebraska, Anderson sat in one of Melton's meetings and thought it was something he could handle.

"When I was a senior in high school I went to a linebackers film session and everyone was asleep, including Coach Melton," Anderson said, laughing "and I thought, 'This is great!'"

Unfortunately for Melton, a heart attack a few months later forced him to retire from coaching at the University of Nebraska at the age of 63 after a 26-year career. To replace Melton, Husker coach Tom Osborne hired a young and fiery protégé of old-school Tennessee coach Johnny Majors. Kevin Steele played at Tennessee in an era when water breaks were seen as a weakness and blood was expected to be seen from time to time.

Other than coaching linebackers, and being human, Steele did not have much in common with Melton. Their film sessions, predictably, were different, too.

"If you were just slouching in Coach Steele's film sessions, he would be there with his red light shining it in your eyes and you might have to stand up," Anderson said. "He was a very good coach and he really drilled the fundamentals into you, but he had his own way."

Anderson learned his basic football fundamentals as a grade-schooler growing up in Wyoming. By junior high he was starting to think about playing college football.

"In seventh grade a kid from my area got a scholarship to Wyoming, and I thought it would be cool to play at Wyoming," Anderson said. "But then I moved to Nebraska and set my sights on that."

Anderson played well enough in high school that Nebraska did come calling on the linebacker with an offer. Going to Nebraska was a done deal by the time Osborne showed up in a memorable 1980s vehicle to make one of his typical pitches.

"Coach Osborne pulled up to my house in his wood panel station wagon," Anderson said. "He just said, 'We would like to have you play for us and we will help you get your degree.' He said if I worked hard, I would have an opportunity to play, no promises."

Working hard was a trait of Anderson's and that opportunity would start in earnest the summer before his freshman year. He was no longer a recruit being wooed by NU, but a football player, and he noticed the difference. Anderson remembered as a recruit he had Cindy Solich, assistant coach Frank Solich's daughter, as a player host and how nice the recruiting visits were in Lincoln.

However, once Anderson was on campus as a student, "the lobster tails, steak, and pretty girls sort of disappeared," he said. They were replaced by a human battering ram and the African American version of a famous chiseled movie star.

"That first camp at Nebraska was an eye-opener," Anderson said. "They bring in the freshmen and junior college transfers before all the older guys, and Omar Soto [junior college fullback] was just lighting people up on play after play but we were only in helmets and shorts.

"Then I thought, 'OK, this is gonna be tough.'"

And when the lettermen showed up, Anderson was further awed.

"Then I saw [linebacker] Pat Tyrance and he looked like Arnold Schwarzenegger with muscles on top of muscles," Anderson said. "I think [offensive lineman] Tom Punt is still feeling one of Tyrance's hits; it was one of those boom hits you never forget.

"Then I thought, 'Okay, this is gonna be *really* tough!'"

Part of that feeling of awe came from being one of so many good players at his position of inside linebacker. At that time in the late 1980s Nebraska played a 5–2 defense with five defensive linemen and two inside linebackers. The outside linebackers would be part of the five-man front on the line of scrimmage.

"There were four inside linebackers in my class and Coach Osborne called us together and said we need one guy to move to outside linebacker," Anderson said. "We were all looking around and one of the guys says, 'I'm the tallest, I'll move.'"

The taller guy was Trev Alberts. He would go on to win the Dick Butkus Award in 1993 as the top linebacker in college football. Also, he would become an All-American in 1993 and get drafted No. 5 overall in the 1994 NFL Draft. But it was not Alberts' accomplishments that made Anderson envious of Alberts at Nebraska in a semi-serious way.

"I sorta regretted not volunteering to move because the outside linebackers coach Tony Samuel was a riot. Every day was a party in practice with him," Anderson said. "We would be getting our brains beat in as inside linebackers, and we would look over at the outside linebackers just having a ball."

Even if he was not Anderson's position coach, Samuel had one positive and one not-so positive comment about Anderson.

"Mike was a tough run-stopper, probably one of the better ones we ever had at Nebraska," Samuel said. "He was very dependable and he started a lot games for us."

However, Mike was not the only Anderson helping the program. Anderson's dad owned a car dealership and was involved in donating cars to the university for coaches to drive, which was a good thing...usually.

"Mike's dad was great to the program and we had the Wheel Club and coaches got free rentals," Samuel said. "I got a car one day from his dad's place on O Street, and I thought it was sorta blue-ish when I picked it up [but] I didn't think too much about it."

However, what he didn't know then was his car was an innovative Taurus that was an amethyst color and would change shades with the light.

"Like I said, it was blue-ish, but when I got to the stadium it was purple-ish, even pink-ish at times. Even the secretaries were ribbing me about it so I took it back," Samuel said laughing. "I'm still very appreciative to Mike's dad, but just that one was different."

Anderson was also showing he was different, too, as the hard work with Steele in practice began to pay off for the linebacker after being a backup as a freshman in 1990. In fall practices before the 1991 season, he was in contention for a starting job.

The 6'1", 230-pounder also helped his caused with his hard work off the field in the weight room. In a team of dedicated college athletes, he was the 1991 Lifter of the Year for the football team. Boyd Epley was in charge of the strength and conditioning program at Nebraska from 1969 to 1995 and is regarded as one of the most important figures, if not the most important person, in college strength and conditioning in the last 50 years.

Epley felt Anderson was an all-star in terms of strength and character.

"Mike Anderson was one of the strongest linebackers to ever play for Nebraska," Epley said. "He was a no-nonsense player, never in trouble, and always worked hard."

In 1991, that work ethic began to pay off when he won a starting job and was second on the team in tackles with 80, trailing only strong safety Steve Carmer with 87. Anderson also caused two fumbles and recovered one fumble for a team that would claim a share of the Big 8 title with Colorado, NU's first since 1988.

Despite the championship, that season did not end well for Nebraska as it lost to Miami 22–0 in the Orange Bowl. That loss, along with previous New Year's Day defeats, helped trigger a bigger picture change in the program. They began to change the defensive system to include more speed on the field at linebacker as the staff reassessed their strategy.

When Anderson came to Nebraska, the Huskers ran a 5–2 front with five defensive linemen and two inside linebackers. In an attempt to get more speed on the field, they began to occasionally use a 4–3 front with another linebacker and one less defensive lineman. But the linebackers flanking the inside guy were going to be bigger safeties to create more opportunity for defensive backs to move up and not the inside linebackers.

"Our defense kind of evolved as we were using the 4–3 in pass defense and stopping the run anyway, so I think they saw a natural progression," Anderson said. "The thinking was let's shift to this and stop the teams with speed like Miami and Florida State. In 1992 maybe we used it half the time, and my senior year it was our base defense."

It did not affect Anderson as much as some other inside linebackers because Anderson was at the top at the position. He did not leave the field when two lighter linebackers would flank him in the new 4–3.

The move paid off. NU would win the Big 8 championship outright in 1992 and Anderson was a key piece of the defense. In 1992 Anderson missed a game due to injury but was still second in tackles for the linebackers and recorded his first sack.

That Anderson was able to transition in the middle of his career to a new defensive front and stay a starter was not surprising to one Husker coach.

"Mike was smart and picked things up quickly. He just needed to see something once. He is the kind of player that makes coaches look smart" said defensive coordinator Charlie McBride. "Also, when he would make a play, he didn't let everyone know it. He just kept his mouth shut and would make another play."

Anderson said McBride was easy to play for at Nebraska. He was the kind of coach who could get on players but they would not take it personally because he had trust with them. They knew he cared for them and was pushing them to be their best.

In fact, the players even tried to pull a prank on him—the atomic sit up—as they had a unique and positive relationship with him. (Note: Google "atomic sit up" if you *really* want to know.)

The coaching staff prepared Anderson well, and his teammates did, too. During the week in practice he routinely faced All-Conference and All-American players. He came out better as a player, albeit occasionally disfigured.

"I still can't bend one of my fingers thanks to Calvin Jones," Anderson said. "I tried to grab him as he ran by and my finger got caught in his jersey and my tendon rolled up into my hand.

"I came off the field and said, 'I think I broke my finger.' I can't remember who the trainer was, but he just told me it wasn't and to get back in there."

Another Husker on offense said Anderson was a textbook linebacker and teammate.

"Mike led by example, he didn't call attention to himself and he was, and still is, a very humble guy," said Husker wingback Clester Johnson Sr., a teammate from 1991 to 1993. "A unique thing about him was whether you were a walk-on freshman or an older starter, you felt you could go to him to talk about anything.

"Successful teams need stand-up guys like that."

Johnson also mentioned physicality was Anderson's calling card and there was evidence to prove it every day.

"I always remember after practice his forehead would be a little bloody from his helmet because he was that physical hitting people," Johnson said. "Practice like you play, that was Mike Anderson. And that prepared us on offense as well because you knew if you locked up with Mike you better be ready or you will get blasted."

The Huskers would be returning many key pieces in Anderson's senior year from a Big 8 championship so expectations were high. The defense was anchored by Anderson, Alberts, linebacker Ed Stewart, and defensive lineman Terry Connealy. The offense was led by quarterback Tommie Frazier and running backs Calvin Jones and Lawrence Phillips.

The 1993 Huskers lived up to those expectations by going undefeated and claiming another Big 8 championship. Anderson would garner all-conference accolades after the season, as well. The Huskers were poised for the national championship game against undefeated No. 1 Florida State.

FSU had defeated NU by two touchdowns in the prior Orange Bowl. In one of the greatest games ever played, heavily favored FSU barely got by Nebraska 18–16.

The game was memorable for other reasons, as well

"During the game the refs were saying, 'Don't touch him, don't touch him' about Charlie Ward [FSU's Heisman-winning quarterback]," Anderson said, "and that is just not normal.

"You got the feeling the refs were for them. So many questionable calls went against us. But [refereeing] is not easy; I just wish they had instant replay back then."

Anderson was the Husker who recovered a Florida State fumble by William Floyd at the 1-yard line in the end zone. On the field the Huskers were sure it was a fumble and replays showed it clearly was a fumble, but a missed call led to seven points in a game decided by two points. Along with a phantom clip call on a NU punt return for a touchdown Nebraska was left with some bitter disappointment after the game.

"I knew in my heart we were going to beat those guys and we should have beaten them," Anderson said.

Even with many curious calls going against them, Nebraska still came close to winning the game. Maybe closer than some people realize since FSU barely converted a fourth-and-1 on a drive that saw them score the go-ahead points late in the 4th quarter. On that play FSU handed the

The 1992 Blackshirts and defensive coaches pose on the beach before the Orange Bowl. Mike Anderson is standing fourth from the right. College Football Hall of Famer Trev Alberts is third from right and Coach McBride is kneeling on the far right. *(Courtesy of Kenny Wilhite)*

ball off to Floyd up the middle and he gained one yard, but the play could have been blown up in the backfield.

"We called a middle blitz that time and it was my responsibility to tell the defensive tackle which way to blitz," Anderson said. "So I told him to go this direction and I followed right behind him and we just missed him. Their guy fell forward for the first down. I wonder what would have happened if I told him to go the other direction? Ya never know...."

FSU was one of the few teams that beat Nebraska while Anderson was a Husker, but the pluses far outweighed the minuses in a college career at Nebraska that started with taking note of physical fullback Omar Soto. But it was another Husker fullback at the end of Anderson's career at whom he would marvel most, though he never let the younger player know about it.

"The hardest hitter I ever went against, in any league, was Cory Schlesinger; his nickname 'Joe Rockhead' fit him well," Anderson said. "The way he could use his body for [the] full amount of power was amazing.

"I didn't go down from his blocks, but he knocked the wind out of me a few times in practice. I never let him know that though."

The two players had another thing in common aside from the fact that when they hit something, it stopped moving.

"Back then, we sorta looked alike and people would confuse us on campus," Anderson said. "So when I turned 21, I gave him my ID."

The Grand Island native would soon reach two more formal milestones by graduating from Nebraska in 1994 and having a professional football career. He spent time with the New York Jets and then in NFL Europe playing for Amsterdam.

Once his professional playing days were over, he came back to Nebraska and took over the family automobile business that provided Samuel with the car. In 2015 the auto dealership is flourishing as Anderson is using the same work ethic he displayed in his Cornhuskers career to expand the business. Anderson owns six auto dealerships under the umbrella name of Anderson Auto Group in Lincoln, Grand Island, and St. Joseph, Missouri.

—Jimmy Sheil

CHAPTER 15

KENNY WILHITE

Cornerback, 1990–92

Name this Husker:

- His enrollment was hastened by a gunshot wound;
- In practice he talked trash to a deaf guy;
- He considers a hug from Husker assistant coach Charlie McBride among his most prized NU memories.

If you guessed Kenny Wilhite, you were probably in the Nebraska Football Recruiting Office—where Wilhite works as the Associate Director of Player Personnel—as this interview was being done, since none of the above are well-known facts.

A well-known fact is that Wilhite was a junior college transfer to Nebraska in 1990 from Dodge City Community College. Although he was a high school star, he ended up at the junior college after not taking academics as seriously as he should have at Oakville High School in St. Louis.

His college career at Nebraska was set to begin in August of that year as a Husker wingback after being a dangerous option quarterback at Dodge. However, an incident at home in the early part of summer made his position at Nebraska the least of his worries and cast some doubt on his career and health overall.

Wilhite grew up in an area of St. Louis that is known for lacking resources and role models. In fact, by the late 1980s the city was almost in freefall, with people and jobs moving to the suburbs in large numbers and freeways being constructed through formerly vibrant neighborhoods, weakening the city's core.

However, Wilhite had a strong family and part of that bond was looking out for each other and holding your own.

"We were not supposed to go looking for trouble, but we were not allowed to back down from a fight either," Wilhite said.

A lingering conflict at the beginning of the summer involving Wilhite's younger brother with an older guy came to a head. On a June afternoon a group came to the family's home looking for trouble, and Wilhite's uncle told Wilhite and his three younger brothers to handle the situation. The brothers listened to their uncle and soon more than fists were flying.

"We went outside and it was on," Wilhite said. "I saw someone hand a guy a gun and he aimed it at my brother. So I yelled at my brother to run and I pushed him right when the guy started shooting and he got me in the arm."

The wound was not life-threatening; however, any shooting is serious and Wilhite's mother wanted him out of that environment as soon as possible. She made a call to Lincoln and asked the staff if her son could come to Lincoln a few months early. The staff said yes without asking for details.

When they got to campus the next day Wilhite did not want to tell head coach Tom Osborne and his primary recruiter, assistant coach Ron Brown, that he had gotten shot. But Wilhite's mother said he needed to tell them what happened. Finally, he relented and laid it out for the coaches, even if Osborne did not get it at first.

"Coach, I got shot yesterday," Wilhite said.

"With a needle?" Osborne replied in all seriousness.

"No coach, with a gun," Wilhite said, fighting back a smirk and then raising up his sleeve to show the scar.

Osborne was a bit taken back and looked at Brown and then looked at Wilhite's mom and had one question for the parent.

"Do you mind if we keep him here and get him graduated?" Osborne asked.

Wilhite's mom could only nod her head in agreement and thanks. Wilhite said right then it re-affirmed that Osborne cared about him as a person, not just as a football player. The player became even more committed to show Osborne, or "The Man" as he and his teammates called him, that he was a quality recruit and person after that day. Wilhite would need that motivation down the road to stick with a rehabilitation program when it would become painful to get back on the field.

The fact that the Dodge City Community College player was talking to Nebraska coaches that day was due to the Cornhuskers staff going the extra mile a few months earlier in the recruiting process. Many colleges were vying for this versatile athlete but it came down to two distinctly different programs—Nebraska and the now defunct Pacific University in California—for the St. Louis native.

In deciding between the two schools, Wilhite had a request that he felt was reasonable, but would be telling about the head coach.

"I told both schools, 'Listen, the head coach needs to come see me at my junior college and then visit my house in St Louis,'" Wilhite said.

Recruiting Wilhite for Pacific was future NFL Super Bowl winning coach Jon Gruden, but he could not get Pacific head coach Walt Harris to make the visit. Wilhite told Brown about his request, as well, and Brown and Osborne showed up at Dodge Community College shortly thereafter.

All through the visit, Osborne graciously signed autographs before departing for Wilhite's home. The two Nebraska coaches flew to St. Louis and they called Wilhite back at his junior college and asked if he had a decision.

"Coach, I'm going to the University of Nebraska," Wilhite said.

That first summer in Lincoln, Wilhite got to know and see firsthand somebody he described as the best athlete he has ever played with on any level. Somebody to whom the tag "freak" gets applied in a complimentary way.

"I come here that summer and we have 7-on-7s at the stadium," Wilhite said. "This big dude walks in and takes off his shirt and he is just cut up and I think to myself, 'Who is that D-lineman?'"

The "big dude" with a thick Southern accent starts talking to anyone who will listen, or even those who weren't listening.

"Hey bro! Bro! Give me the ball. Just give me the ball," said a

Kenny Wilhite (left) with his defensive coordinator, Charlie McBride, in the Nebraska football offices in 2015. Wilhite works in those offices as the Associate Director of Player Personnel for coach Mike Riley. *(Courtesy of Kenny Wilhite)*

strutting Johnnie Mitchell said, as the 6'5", 250-pound tight end was warming up to play.

Mitchell then proceeded to make nonstop plays with speed uncommon for a tight end, especially given his size. His All-Conference hands were snatching passes left and right. But the athletic show was not done yet that afternoon during those 7-on-7s at the stadium.

During a break in the passing scrimmage, Mitchell saw Wilhite on the sideline and went up to him to ask him a question.

"You a quarterback?" Mitchell asked, looming over Wilhite even though he probably knew the answer.

Wilhite was slightly put off by Mitchell's manner but replied yes, he was a quarterback. Wilhite really did not like Mitchell's response.

"I bet my arm is stronger than yours," Mitchell said.

Wilhite was irritated and offended as an athlete. However, after Mitchell threw the ball 65 yards with his right hand—and then 65 yards with his left hand—Wilhite just shrugged and did not even take his throw.

A summer back injury and the still-healing gunshot wound made it necessary for Wilhite to redshirt for the 1990 season. It gave him time to weigh his options, and he decided he was not going to be playing quarterback at Nebraska. He opted to stay on the offensive side of the ball, with his speed and ability to make plays with his hands, and he settled in at wingback in the first month of the 1990 season.

Just because Wilhite was redshirting in 1990 did not mean he would not help the team during an important week with game preparation. Wilhite's experience at quarterback allowed Osborne to utilize him in another way to help the team. For one week he moved back to quarterback to help Nebraska prepare for its biggest game of 1990 versus defending Big 8 champion Colorado.

At that time running the show for No. 9 Colorado was option whiz Darian Hagan, who incidentally later in life would become good friends with Wilhite through their CFL playing days after college. (In the CFL, Wilhite would play four years, including an All-Star season in 1995, and finish third in Player of the Year voting behind Doug Flutie.)

For that week Wilhite would run the Colorado offense on the scout team as Hagan. The junior college quarterback would be going up against such Blackshirt stars as inside linebacker Pat Tyrance, outside linebacker Mike Croel, and deaf defensive lineman Kenny Walker, who would go on to make the All-American team after the 1990 season.

"I'm mimicking Hagan in a scrimmage and the first four plays versus the Blackshirts, I was untouched and Charlie Mac just loses it," Wilhite said, laughing. "He told them to get off the field. He screamed at them, 'If you let this guy do this to you, what do you think is gonna happen on Saturday with Colorado?'"

McBride also let another Husker coach know what was going on at the other end of the field with the first-team offense.

"Hey Tom, you need a QB?" McBride yelled to Osborne. "Well, he is down here kicking our ass; we haven't touched the little shit!"

As McBride was screaming, Wilhite could see the defensive guys listening to the assistant coach with hands on hips, breathing deeply and fuming. The next play in the scrimmage started out well for Wilhite, but then....

"On the very next play, we are running the option again and I make my read right and cut up with daylight ahead of me," Wilhite said, "but then out of nowhere Kenny Walker just ear-holes me from the side. My world went sideways and then silent as he slammed me to the ground! Hard too.

"Now, Kenny is deaf, but he was just one of the guys and that's how he wanted to be treated. I was sorta woozy for a second on the ground after that hit from him, but then I popped up. And I knew Kenny could lip read real good, so I said to him, 'Dang Kenny! You let McBride yell at you and then you take it out on me!'"

Walker was not going to let a younger Husker talk to him that way, teammate or not.

"I had hardly finished saying that and BAM! He smacks me upside the helmet! I was a redshirt so I just took it with a laugh and went back to the huddle," Wilhite said. "But I had never had more fun playing football that week as and the Blackshirts couldn't touch me.

"Or hardly touched me, I guess."

Wilhite's work did help the Cornhuskers versus the Buffs that Saturday even if Nebraska did not get the win that week. The Blackshirts kept Colorado off the board until the fourth quarter and actually had a 12–0 lead, but the fourth quarter saw a big Colorado comeback and NU lost 27–12.

As Nebraska finished the regular season in 1990, the staff saw that for the next year they might have some holes on defense in the secondary.

In fact, defensive backs coach George Darlington, with whom Wilhite had some run-ins in practice over the player being too aggressive in drills, had requested Wilhite for the defense.

Darlington saw many of the same things another defensive coach did in Wilhite.

"Kenny is a corner; he had all the things you look for in a cornerback," McBride said. "He had great quickness and good speed, but the one thing that separated him from other guys who were good athletes was he was a good tackler. He was tough; he would hit you and wrap you up."

While he had the tools for either side of the ball, Wilhite was content playing on offense. But a need on defense left him with two good options. He decided to move to defense, but he did have some initial concerns.

"I hadn't backpedaled since high school," Wilhite said. "I knew I could play, [but I needed to learn] the small things on being a DB. I watched [starters] Curtis Cotton and Tyrone Legette every practice after that."

Wilhite made the move during bowl preparations in 1990 as the Huskers prepared to meet Georgia Tech in the Citrus Bowl. It was a roller coaster at times, as he was just getting the hang of the position, but he did well enough to consider the move permanent as they headed into spring of 1991. In spring practices he got off to a quick start while covering one of NU's better receivers.

"The first play of live scrimmage in the spring I was covering Jon Bostick and I got a pick," Wilhite said. "I always remind my guy, J.B., of that one."

Wilhite continued his strong play into fall camp in 1991 and seemed all set; however, he did not have a nickname. Some of his teammates, led by Bostick, would soon take care of this.

"Kenny didn't have a nickname when he got moved up to the big boy locker room," Bostick said. "We went by his locker and he had a bunch of high school prom pics up with his big afro almost as big as him and a 1970s tux, so that got us thinking.

"I'm sure he wanted a cool nickname, like 'Prime Time' or 'Wilhite Island,' being a DB. But we decided on "Pip," after Gladys Knight and the Pips. Kenny with that prom look was not a front man yet, but still very important to our team."

Wilhite, or "Pip," was indeed important as he had worked himself into the secondary's regular rotation for the season opener despite not being a starter. The staff told him he would go into the game in the second series for Curtis Cotton and the fourth series for Tyrone Legette.

Wilhite validated the coaches' trust in their new cornerback in the non-conference season in 1991. After playing his junior college career on offense, he showed he wanted the ball in his hands again with an impressive start on the defensive side of the ball. Wilhite got an interception in his first game versus Utah State, then another versus Colorado State. He ran the streak to three with a pick versus eventual 1991 National Champion, Washington, although NU dropped that game 36–21 as UW mounted a second-half comeback.

Aside from the Washington loss, the season hit a minor bump when Wilhite suffered a shoulder injury in practice during the Kansas State week. Defensive backs coach Darlington said Wilhite would only be used in an emergency situation and no emergency was expected versus the lightly regarded Wildcats. To boot, Nebraska hadn't lost to Kansas State since 1968.

However, that day KSU went toe-to-toe with NU. In a back-and-forth game, the Huskers led late in the fourth quarter, but the Wildcats were driving to tie the game and potentially win with a 2-point conversion. Coach Darlington made a decision to help stop the Wildcats' passing game.

Wilhite was on the sideline still as KSU drove into Huskers territory. The always confident cornerback was banged up and did not have his usual confidence, but he was ready to go in if called.

"KSU was inside our 10 with under a minute left and Coach D finally sent me into the game," Wilhite said. "It was maybe one of the few times I have been nervous in sports as I was just not 100 perent, but they had me prepared to make a play."

And he would have to make a play as Kansas State threw to Wilhite's guy for the possible game-tying touchdown. But Wilhite was up to the challenge, and on his only play of the 38–31 NU victory, he batted the ball away.

Wilhite was healed and ready to go the next week and the season was going well. He had four interceptions going into the Kansas game in mid-November, in which he had two interceptions, but the last came at a great cost. He intercepted a pass versus the Jayhawks and started going up field when bad luck struck.

As Wilhite was returning the interception, he made a cut and tore his ACL. His season was done. Wilhite would still make All-Big 8 as a defensive back in 1991, but it was almost his last season of football.

ACL injuries are sometimes career-ending. At the time in 1991 they usually required one calendar year of rehab. What made matters worse for Wilhite was that he had already used his redshirt year and his eligibility clock was likely up in 1992, so he needed to have an almost unheard-of rehabilitation time from the injury.

As Wilhite began his rehab, he got to know NU trainer Doak Ostergard well. Ostergard was an innovative trainer responsible for many advancements and tools for rehabilitation, such as the shoulder harness. But the all-important rehabilitation process didn't start well for Wilhite.

"In rehab for my knee I got so frustrated and depressed because it hurt so bad. I just could not take it anymore," Wilhite said. "And I went home and told my grandma that it was too much for me and I'm quitting."

Wilhite's grandmother was not on the same page as her grandson. She had her own way of telling him it wasn't really about football and he needed to turn around and go back to NU.

Now.

"Your black ass better get back up there and apologize to those people because I know you cussed them out," Wilhite's grandmother guessed, correctly. "One thing they can't do is take away that piece of paper [degree] from you. Football will be over one day, but they can't take that piece of paper away from you."

Wilhite trudged back to Lincoln and apologized to Ostergard. The trainer let him know why he was pushing him so hard. At the end of the 1991 season Osborne told Ostergard that his number one priority, if possible, was getting Wilhite back into playing shape for the Huskers for the next season.

However, just because "The Man" asks for something doesn't mean it will happen. Wilhite overcame the early obstacles in rehab and stuck with the process. He began to make some progress and was back on the field for spring ball. His recovery was aided by McBride's encouragement and optimism, even if Wilhite did not have as much confidence as the assistant coach.

"Charlie believed in you even when you didn't believe in yourself," Wilhite said. "He could yell at you and get tobacco all in your face, but you knew he cared for you so you could take it. He was just pushing because he believed in you."

McBride was an assistant coach in college football from 1966 to 1999, and he said Wilhite was not your average player. In fact, McBride said, Wilhite was unique in his demeanor as well as his ability.

"Kenny was always smiling and never let things bug him," McBride said. "Now, he was a great athlete too, but he had a competitor's mindset. There might be challenges along the way but he would not stop giving effort to be successful. He is still the same way today."

That determination and mindset helped Wilhite get back on the field for the 1992 season. Nebraska was looking to win the Big 8 championship outright since it had shared the crown with Colorado the year before. NU was well-stocked on both sides of the ball; the only question

Blackshirt Kenny Wilhite covers Husker split end Matt Turman in 1992 before Turman moved to quarterback. *(Courtesy of Kenny Wilhite)*

mark for Nebraska was not having an All-Conference candidate at the most important position on the field—quarterback. However, that situation would take care of itself as the year progressed.

In 1992 Wilhite witnessed the emergence of maybe the best and most important Husker of all time in quarterback Tommie Frazier. By mid-year, the lanky true freshman had ascended to the top of the depth chart after playing sparingly in the non-conference schedule. Frazier began to emerge during his first start early in the conference schedule versus Missouri.

Wilhite said the team knew Frazier could play; he was obviously fast and a true maestro at running the option, but his toughness is what got Wilhite's attention versus Colorado. Also, the game gave the team an idea about the program's future with the signal-caller from Bradenton, Florida.

"Against Colorado, Tommie got hit so hard by Deon Figures," Wilhite said. "And Figures was 6'2", 210, just ripped up and Deon was about to get drafted in the first round of the NFL Draft too. I mean, Tommie got rocked by Figures and Tommie just jumped up after that hit and practically got in his face like, 'Was that your best shot?'

"Right then and there I knew we had a soldier in T-Fraz. We were ready to roll with him!"

Wilhite said those types of competitors are needed to win championships, and NU would not have won the Big 8 in 1992 without Frazier. Wilhite felt when he arrived at Nebraska in 1990 that they had a few of those type of guys, but they needed more to take the program to the next level.

"I always reflect back to this when thinking about football players," Wilhite said. "How many of these guys would I take with me to a brawl back in my neighborhood in St. Louis? By the time I was done, I just saw more of those types of guys at Nebraska."

Wilhite said it was not all about ability or strength in football as sometimes there is a toughness test that needs to be passed.

"I'll tell you what, even in pro football, there are guys that can lift all the weights in the gym, but if they get their bell rung, they check out. They are done," Wilhite said. "We needed more guys like Miami and FSU had—cats that were just stone-cold that would go through a wall for each other.

"Besides Tommie, it was guys like Dwayne Harris, Barron Miles, Corey Dixon, and Cory Schlesinger. Schlesinger would hit you, boy! Rockhead was a good nickname for him. By the way, this might surprise some people, but I would take Tom Hesse to a scrap with me too. Farm boy and all. That dude took some shots in the Citrus Bowl versus Georgia Tech, but he kept coming."

That Colorado game in which Frazier showed he was up to the task was the first rout of back-to-back ranked teams in October 1992 by Nebraska. Aside from the blowouts, those games had something else in common—both opponents got the Huskers' attention before the games with their mouths.

"We read things in the paper, bulletin board material from both Colorado and KU before we played them," Wilhite said. "Colorado said they were not going to let a frosh QB beat them and KU said they were going to come in here to Lincoln and beat us, so both times we just beat the sleeves off them."

While both opponents reportedly kept their sleeves on, both games were over by halftime. Nebraska beat Colorado 52–7 and then the following week beat the Jayhawks 49–7. But for all the conference highs in 1992, there was a low.

Lowly Iowa State, with a 3–6 record, derailed any late NU National Championship hopes by beating the Huskers in Ames. A name that elicits pain, and some laughter, 20 years later is Iowa State quarterback Marv Seiler. He broke free for a possible two-score lead late in the game but Wilhite chased him down and prevented him from scoring while trying to strip him. Unfortunately, it only delayed the ending.

"I made the tackle on the quarterback and I caught him at the 4-yard line," Wilhite said, "but I tried to strip him for the last 10 yards of the run. The ball wasn't coming out; he had it wrapped up tight."

Iowa State scored a few plays later to ice the game. Losing to a team with a losing record was a first for Osborne, and on the bus back to Lincoln Wilhite had a first of his own. Upset over the embarrassing loss to the Cyclones, Wilhite would try something to numb the pain on the bus ride home.

"For the first time, and the last time, I tried chew on that bus home from Ames, but I didn't know the chew I got was laced with liquor," Wilhite said. "Halfway home I took it out but it was too late, I was feeling it the whole way home."

While the Iowa State game was a downer for Wilhite in 1992, his team would clinch the Big 8 championship outright later in the season with victories over Oklahoma and Kansas State. For the second year in a row, Wilhite was a major contributor to a conference-winning and Orange Bowl–bound team.

Those accomplishments helped Wilhite get the attention of the pros. He had a stint with the Chicago Bears but ended up in the Canadian Football League. While there, he embraced a role that Nebraska was a little leery to have him take on with his injuries.

"Kenny went up north and he had a nice CFL career," Samuel said. "And he was a heck of a return man up there but we were a bit hesitant to turn him loose with his knee in 1992. But he could have done it."

Wilhite played four years in the CFL for four teams: the Sacramento Gold Miners, the San Antonio Texans, the Ottawa Rough Riders, and the Hamilton Tiger Cats. He was an All-Star in 1996 with Ottawa. That year he finished third in the Player of the Year voting with Doug Flutie winning the award.

While Wilhite made many big plays in the CFL and as a Husker in games, maybe the biggest play he made post–Dodge City Community

College might not have been versus an opponent, but in spring practices in 1992 when he was trying to get healthy, both physically and mentally.

The rehab process that spring was stuck in neutral, so to speak, as camp was coming to a close.

"Coming off my ACL tear, there were doubts about me in spring ball. I probably had some too about myself," Wilhite said. "I had a big bulky brace on and I didn't get many reps as spring ball was going along. I was getting eased back into action and [you] just don't know sometimes with injuries."

But then Wilhite made a play in a scrimmage and McBride was right there.

"I got a pick on Trumane Bell on a fade route in the end zone and the first guy to me was Charlie and he gave me a big ol' hug," Wilhite said, smiling with a slight lump in his throat. "Then he yelled at me, 'I told them! I told them they can't count you out! I told them!'

"Charlie Mac...that's my guy!"

—*Jimmy Sheil*

CHAPTER 16

JAY FOREMAN

Linebacker, 1994–98

Only a handful of Nebraska Cornhuskers can claim to be a member of three of the prestigious program's five national championships. One of those players who can boast three championship rings—in 1994, 1995, and 1997—is linebacker Jay Foreman, the son of former NFL great Chuck Foreman.

Jay was born in Eden Prairie, Minnesota, in 1976. From the time Jay was about 18 months old until he was six or seven he was raised by his grandparents in Frederick, Maryland. During his developmental years, he returned to Minnesota, where he played football in high school for Mike Grant, the son of Bud Grant, Chuck's coach with the Minnesota Vikings.

From the time he was a young boy growing up in suburban Minneapolis, Jay was well aware of the legend of Chuck Foreman. As he told the *Minnesota Daily* in 1997, he didn't know whether his name was Jay Foreman or "Chuck Foreman's kid."

"It's something I'll never be able to get rid of," Jay Foreman said. "Every time I saw my name written when I was in high school, there was always a comma after it and then my dad's name. I don't want to say I didn't like it, but I didn't know why I couldn't have my own identity."

Jay Foreman wasted no time in developing his own identity when he arrived on the Nebraska campus in 1994, his first of five seasons with the Cornhuskers program.

He redshirted that first season but was still instrumental in the 1994 national championship team that defeated Miami in the Orange Bowl to give coach Tom Osborne his first of three national titles.

Foreman earned a starting role for the 1995 season, which included the second straight national championship with the famous 62–24 rout of Florida in the Fiesta Bowl. In his first two seasons in the program, Foreman hadn't experienced a loss.

"When the Florida game came and we finally got to play them, we had a point to prove," Foreman said. "I think that year coaches let us know we were playing for something more than just a national championship. We were playing for dominance."

Part of that dominance included quieting a Florida team that had failed miserably in trying to intimidate Nebraska during pregame warm-ups. Several Gator players ran over and through the Cornhuskers' side of the field, kicked helmets, and caused a general stir.

"That was probably the worst thing they could've done," Foreman said. "Once they did that, it was going to be something personal. We didn't take our foot off the pedal.

"They were doing a lot of talking and we definitely had a bunch of guys who weren't going to back down from anybody. They tried to intimidate us, but we weren't going to be intimidated. We were number one. We were the defending champions. That let me know they were scared, that they knew they weren't going to beat us."

Once the game started and a physical Nebraska team exerted its will against a finesse Florida team, Foreman quickly discovered something.

"You just kind of realized these guys aren't even that good. After the first couple of initial hits, you're like, 'Wow, these guys are softer than our scout team,'" Foreman said. "Right then, as long as we didn't give the game away with busted coverages and stuff like that, I knew—I wouldn't say it would be an easy game but a game that we should win."

Eden Prairie, Minnesota, is not known as the football capital of the United States, so it's not surprising that Foreman wasn't heavily recruited out of high school. Chuck Foreman had played running back at the University of Miami, and Jay thought he might follow in his father's footsteps. His home-state school, the Minnesota Gophers, reportedly showed no interest, even though Jay was an All-State player as a senior, rushing for 950 yards and 14 touchdowns and making 43 tackles and two interceptions as a defensive back. "The Gophers, to be quite blunt, don't know what they are doing," Jay once told the *Minnesota Daily.*

"Miami, Michigan, and Nebraska offered me a scholarship to play defense, but not the Gophers. I don't understand how they said I couldn't play at their university, where if they win three games a year, it's like a national championship."

However, Nebraska assistant coach Dan Young saw talent in the high school senior and called him every Monday night at 6:15 PM to ask how Jay's game went and how he was doing. On his first recruiting trip to Nebraska, after seeing the academics, the facilities, and the campus, Jay knew he had found his home as a Husker. It was a perfect match.

Foreman redshirted his first season. He was thankful not to play running back, because Nebraska was stacked at the position. He also didn't have the size for blocking as a wingback. (Eden Prairie didn't have strength coaches and weight rooms.) So he bided his time and learned, grew stronger, and honed his skills. Every single practice he got better and he grew in confidence.

One player instrumental in Foreman's development during his redshirt season, he said, was Clint Brown, a senior walk-on linebacker from Arlington, Nebraska, who played behind starter Troy Dumas on the Cornhuskers' 1994 national championship team.

Brown, Foreman said, has as much of an influence on his career as anyone within the Nebraska program.

"He was behind Dumas but he knew I wanted to learn," Foreman said. "He knew I wanted to be better. He had no problem taking me under his wing. He was taking me in the weight room and working me out. He put me in the position to get to the next level. That had a huge influence on me.

"That's how you get championship teams. You have the All-Americans on the field, but you have guys who are the nuts and bolts behind the scenes, too."

In the 1995 Spring Game, Foreman admits he was scared to death, facing veteran players like Grant Wistrom and brothers Christian and

Jay Foreman (left) with fellow NFL players Keith Newman, Shawn Bryson, and Brian O'Neal. *(Courtesy of Jay Foreman)*

Jason Peter—also known as the "Peterbuilt Brothers," a huge, imposing, and intimidating duo.

But in that first game, Foreman learned he could hold his own. During many plays against the offense, the defense didn't hold back against its fellow teammates, and the glorified scrimmage was rough. Yet in that one game, Foreman gained the confidence that would support him for the rest of his career. He said that even in the pros, when his confidence was shaken, he could remember that Spring Game and how he felt knowing he could conquer anything.

"Everybody wanted to compete so well," Foreman said of his time with the Cornhuskers. "The funny thing is when you watch that team and you watch a run play or a pass play there were literally, every single play, eight guys to the ball. We wanted to make sure we got our hits in. That's how thick the competition was. We had to go out there 100 percent all the time."

Foreman remembers sitting on the sideline at the Oklahoma State game when teammate Mike Minter got in his face. Minter was taunting Jay, asking, "Are you soft? Are you going to punk out?" Jay said freshmen were to be seen and not heard, so he tried to remain quiet.

Even with a national championship on the line every week, the smack talk continued. Minter got the best of Foreman, who defiantly took off his helmet and yelled, "Let's go! I will show you!" Minter walked away. Foreman said he realized later that Minter was checking to see if Jay was mentally tough, if he was ready. Jay knew he was, and now, so did Mike Minter.

Defensive coordinator Charlie McBride had his own challenge for Foreman in a practice leading up to that Thursday night game at Oklahoma State, a nationally televised game on ESPN to kick off the 1995 season.

"He comes up to me and looks at me, and I'm like, 'What the hell did I do?'" Foreman said. "He looks at me and he's like, 'Hey, if you don't go out there and hit somebody, if you don't kick some ass, I'm going to knock you out and your damn teeth are going to look like mine.' And he had dentures."

McBride, of course, was merely trying to loosen up Foreman, who'd be making his first career start in his first college game, and on a team loaded with defensive talent. He wanted Foreman to know that he belonged.

"He told me, 'You've had a million reps; you are the best guy at the position. You've deserved it. Don't look over your shoulder. Go out there and handle your business like you have every day in practice and you'll play well,'" Foreman said.

Foreman did, too. On Oklahoma State's first play from scrimmage, the Cowboys ran an iso, Foreman blew up the fullback and was credited with an assisted tackle, along with Minter.

"That's when I knew, 'I can play with these guys,'" Foreman said. "I wasn't going to get beat physically. I wasn't going to let that happen. Second, I wanted to make sure I was going to play hard."

His success made it very comfortable to embrace and ultimately honor the legend of his father. According to the *Minnesota Daily*, Foreman decided to trade his initial jersey number, 56, for 44—the number Chuck Foreman wore as the Vikings' All-Pro running back in the 1970s.

The number 44 became available after the graduation of middle linebacker Jon Hesse. According to the *Daily*, Foreman said he requested the change as a way to honor his father, who raised his son as a single parent. "Growing up," Foreman said, "all we had was each other. It was like we were brothers. I owe him a lot. I asked him after the bowl game about wearing 44, and he said he would like it if I did."

Foreman attributes his success as a Husker to being very competitive. He said he knew the game well, which gave him a mental advantage and that he would give whatever it took to win. In winning back-to-back national championships, Foreman credits the "greatest team around," recalling many phenomenal players like Wistrom and Jason Peter. He jokingly referred to Mike Brown as 'The Black Leprechaun.' He said Brown was always in position and just instinctively knew where the ball was going. Brown was a savvy player—one of the smartest. Foreman called Christian Peter one of his toughest teammates. Physically intimidating and mentally tough, Christian was a leader and didn't even realize it because his mental toughness was contagious.

"The coaches had the easiest job," Foreman said. "The players on the team, the older guys, they policed the team. That leadership goes underappreciated. Very rarely do you find a team where you get 100 percent of the guys all in. And if you're not all in and you can't handle it, you won't cut it. It's like, 'This is the way it is, this is the way you're going to do it, and if you don't do it, you're going to struggle.'"

Foreman boasts that the fans in Nebraska are the most supportive anywhere. He still laughs that only in Nebraska would fans ask for a forecasted national championship so families could plan their vacations around the big game.

His success with the Cornhuskers prepared him to be a fifth-round NFL Draft pick. In his first year with the Buffalo Bills, a starter had an unfortunate injury, giving Foreman the opportunity to prove himself. Once again exceeding expectations, Foreman's confidence and competitive edge turned that opportunity into eight years playing for the Buffalo Bills, Houston Texans, New York Giants, and San Francisco 49ers. He said playing for Nebraska taught him to be a professional. He learned life lessons such as how to bear down, sacrifice for the greater good, and how to go the extra mile.

Today, Foreman has translated this work ethic into forming a successful nonprofit, The Foreman Foundation, which helps diabetics get the medical equipment needed. Jay knows first-hand that having diabetes is not cheap, as many of his family members, including his father, are living with the disease. His company assists by writing grants to find funds to pay for diabetic supplies. His organization also partners with the American Diabetes Association to disseminate information about the illness and how to live a healthy lifestyle.

Jay still lives in Nebraska with his two daughters, who he claims are his inspiration for achievement. Chuck Foreman should be proud to be the father of Jay Foreman.

—*George Achola*

CHAPTER 17

MATT DAVISON

Split End, 1997–2000

He was the last Nebraska Cornhusker to head to the team bus that cool evening on November 8, 1997, at Faurot Field in Columbia, Missouri.

Freshman split end Matt Davison had a legitimate excuse for running behind. From the moment he exited the doors of the visitor's locker room, underneath the southeast corner of the stadium, Davison answered question after question after question.

"I remember walking out of the locker room, and all the lights and cameras under the concourse there at the field were just blinding," Davison said. "There was so much media there, and they all wanted to talk to me."

Thus began Davison's claim to Cornhuskers fame that exists to this day—and will for eternity.

For without Davison's miraculous, diving, shoe-string reception of a ball deflected off teammate Shevin Wiggins' foot, Nebraska wouldn't score a touchdown to force overtime that day against heavy underdog Missouri.

Scott Frost wouldn't dart and bounce his way into the end zone for the go-ahead touchdown. Grant Wistrom and Mike Rucker, both Missouri natives, wouldn't sack quarterback Corby Jones on fourth down to seal a scintillating 45–38 victory.

There is no unbeaten season, no Orange Bowl rout of Peyton Manning-led Tennessee, no shared national championship.

Davison saved the day—and the season.

That's why the teenager from Tecumseh, Nebraska, who grew up watching Cornhuskers football and lauding Tom Osborne, figured if there was ever a time he'd receive some love from the legendary coach, this would be it.

Osborne, always stoic and always reserved, was never quick with effusive praise. He expected good play. He expected consistent play. That should be the norm. Players knew that, too, and responded as such. It's among many reasons Osborne won 255 games over 25 years.

Matt Davison (left) talks with his former coach, Tom Osborne, at a Creating Captains event in 2012. *(Courtesy of Ali Grindle)*

Davison learned this when Osborne came to Tecumseh High School during Davison's senior year to watch him play basketball.

For Osborne, of course, walking into any high school gym in Nebraska is a big deal. He sat with Davison's mother and father. Tecumseh played Elmwood-Murdock, and Davison scored 31 points in victory. Typically a good free-throw shooter, Davison missed four that night in 11 attempts.

"Coach was waiting after the game to meet with me," Davison said, "and I walk into the room—and again, I'm thinking, I played pretty good, we won the game, I had 31 points. I'm thinking, 'Man this is a good game for Coach to see.'

"He taught me a lesson. Right when I walked into the room, the first thing he said to me was, 'Well, Matt, looks like you need to work on those free throws a little bit.' That kind of let me know right away the level of excellence that was going to be demanded at the next level."

Be precise. Play hard every play. Know where to be on every play. Offer no excuses.

"Little things like that, that he says or that he does, are small things that players never forget," Davison said. "For the thousands of players that came through the program, everybody probably has a Tom Osborne story like that, where every time he spoke, you felt yourself really listening hard because you never knew if he was going to say something that you may never forget."

That's kind of how Davison felt when he was the last player to set foot on the team bus after the catch that became known as "The Fleakicker." Everybody else had already boarded. Equipment was stowed away. Osborne occupied his usual seat along the aisle on the front right of the bus.

"I'm a little bit amped to get on the bus, because I hadn't seen Coach Osborne after the game," Davison said. "Once we got to overtime and won, I was standing there with him and everything, but it's not like he was going to turn around during the game and say, 'Hey, great job.' I hadn't really spoken to him. I hadn't seen him after the game at all.

"I'm walking to the bus, and I'm thinking, 'Boy, if there's ever a time I'm going to get a little bit of a pat on the back from the legendary coach that I've revered my whole life, it's going to be right now.' So I'm like, 'What's he going to say?' And as I walk up the stairs, I'm the last one on the bus, he looks up and he just goes, 'Nice catch, Matt.' And he looked right back down."

And that was it.

"For many years after that, whenever I would see coach Osborne, he would always start with, 'Nice catch, Matt. So, what's going on?' He's probably said that to me 100 times, where he just starts the conversation with, 'Nice catch, Matt.' It's kind of become our funny inside joke."

It's possible because of a play Osborne chose at the last moment to cap a remarkable last-minute drive. Nebraska, in just 55 seconds and with no timeouts, had covered 55 yards and faced third-and-10 at the

Missouri 12-yard line with seven seconds remaining. The Huskers, with no time to huddle, used hand signals the entire drive.

"Even though we didn't have to throw the ball much, we practiced our two-minute drill as much as any other team, I suppose. We just didn't have to do it much," Davison said. "I would say we were as prepared as we could be for a team that wasn't put in that situation too many times."

Communication was flawless. Wide receivers coach Ron Brown would signal the plays in, and the wide receivers would get the call, along with Frost and running back Ahman Green. The linemen needed only to worry about their blocking schemes.

On the first play of the drive, split end Kenny Cheatham hauled in a 27-yard pass down the sideline to immediately put Nebraska into Missouri territory and provide a glimmer of hope. Two plays later, Davison caught a ball on a comeback route to gain 13 yards on third-and-10. Cheatham caught two more passes. Nebraska chipped away.

"I do remember fatigue was starting to set in. It was a long drive with no breaks," Davison said. "The play right before I caught the pass, I thought I was interfered with, down by the goal line. So I probably complained a little too much after that play and spent too much energy complaining."

That set up the final play. With the clock stopped because of an incomplete pass, Davison ran across the field to the Nebraska sideline, where players gathered around Osborne, who was deciding what play to run. His choices were "Shotgun 99 double slant," or an option play to the left.

"We were at the 12-yard line, so it would've been risky to run a running play," Davison said. "But they were trying to decide quickly what play to run, and finally coach just said, 'Okay, let's go 99 double slant.'"

The play was one players knew well. The practiced it every day, yet Davison recalls running it only once in his entire career. It was this day, and it wasn't even executed properly.

"Remember, I ran across the field, got the play, then ran all the way back across the field, and if you watch right before the play is snapped,

Matt Davison with his daughter, Reece, and Matt Damon at *The Tonight Show* in 2013. *(Courtesy of Matt Davison)*

I'm barely set," Davison said. "The play clock was running down. It had been a long drive, and I remember being tired."

Frost was supposed to throw to the left side, to either Davison or Lance Brown. He felt those receivers were too closely covered. So back to the right he went. He found a small window and rifled a low pass to Wiggins.

"Frost over the middle…diving…touchdown, Nebraska! Davison on the deflection!"

Nebraska fans know those words by heart from ABC play-by-play announcer Brent Musburger describing Davison's diving grab of a ball off Wiggins' foot. He scored a touchdown, and Kris Brown's extra point forced overtime.

Davison never wavered then, he never has, and he never will. He's convinced he slipped his hands underneath the football and made a clean catch. No doubts. None.

"I knew that I caught it, and that's why I showed it to the officials," Davison said. "When I rolled over, I got up, and in that split second you're thinking, 'I've got to show him the ball. I got to sell it.' I did catch it. I knew I caught it. Luckily, they called it a touchdown. If they called it a trap, the season's lost."

That Davison caught that ball should be of no surprise. After all, catching a football was the easiest task for Davison of any sport he ever played. That included basketball, his true love. It's the sport he felt he would play in college. Colorado State offered him a chance to play basketball, along with football. Kansas State was the first to offer him a spot in football. Wyoming followed, as did Southwest Missouri State.

Those offers disappeared the summer before Davison's senior year of high school, when Nebraska offered a scholarship. Schools knew that's where Davison would go, and they were right.

He arrived in Lincoln weighing all of 170 pounds. Nebraska, meanwhile, had been churning out conference championships and national championships. Davison figured if things went right, he might play by his third or fourth year in the program.

But when he began practicing, he realized he could do one thing better than anybody else in his position group.

He could catch a football.

"We didn't throw it much, but when we did it was through play-action," Davison said. "So typically you were open, and they needed a guy that was reliable."

The first day of two-a-day practices, Davison, playing on the scout team, absorbed a crushing blow on a slant route from Blackshirt corner-back Joe Walker. They weren't wearing pads. The unforgettable jolt left Davison wondering if he might be stuck on the scout team for years to come, despite his soft hands.

He was wrong. The next day, coaches advanced Davison to the number two offense. By the fourth day, he was with the top unit.

In those days, Nebraska divided the team into locker rooms on opposite sides of Memorial Stadium. Throughout fall camp, scholarship players stayed in the locker room underneath South Stadium, and freshmen, redshirts, walk-ons, and some other non-traveling players were in locker rooms underneath North Stadium, in the old Schulte Fieldhouse.

Not until the end of August did coaches fill vacant lockers in South Stadium, held by the previous year's seniors, with new scholarship players who would be playing. The Tuesday before Nebraska's 1997 season opener, coaches met with Davison, and together they determined he would play as a true freshman.

Davison remembers the walk from the freshman locker room to the varsity locker room.

"When they call your name and you're moving into that locker room," he said, "it's a big deal."

The main locker room was split into offense and defense. When Davison walked in, he discovered no available lockers near the wide receivers, running backs, and quarterbacks. He'd have to find a spot on the defensive side of the locker room. His entire freshman season, he lockered next to Chad Kelsay. On the other side of Kelsay were Jason Peter and Grant Wistrom.

"Here I am, a 170-pound freshman, going into the varsity locker room," Davison said, "and they're all looking at me like, 'Who is this kid?' Jason Peter gave me a nickname, 'Pence' which was short for pencil.

"I remember him thinking I was either a punter or a kicker. 'What are you doing on this side of the locker room? What are you doing over here? The kickers and punters are over there.' And I was like, 'No, I play wide receiver,' and I think everybody was shocked that I got moved down to that locker room. 'Why are you down here then, because you're not going to play.'"

But Davison did. He entered the second play of the season's first game, against Akron, when coaches sent him in with the play call. Later in that drive, with the Cornhuskers facing a fourth-and-4, Osborne called a passing play for Davison, who caught the ball to convert a first down.

It led to a touchdown. It also gave coaches enough faith in Davison to throw to him more often.

"I had three catches for 65 yards in my first game ever, and a week prior to that I thought I might redshirt," Davison said. "Everything really happened quickly."

Davison saw the field immediately, not because he was the fastest or strongest player but because he knew how to play. His football IQ allowed him to learn the offense quickly. He knew who to block, where to be, and why.

"I don't recall having any mental errors on the field where I ran the wrong route or blocked the wrong guy or whatever it was," he said. "I learned the playbook quickly, and that comes from as a little kid growing up, watching football constantly. I was just a sports junkie. I watched basketball and football all the time on television. I didn't play video games. I wasn't a kid who could sit in front of a video game for hours on end. I was always playing. I was always watching games.

"As a wide receiver I knew angles, I knew geometry, so I knew how to get open. Little nuances within a route. I knew how to lean into a guy or I knew where I wanted to go and he didn't. I could always seem to get separation. More than anything, I think I just understood the game well."

He credits Brown for his successful career, which ended with 93 receptions for 1,456 yards, two Big 12 championships, and one national championship. Whereas Osborne was a "Steady Eddie" and coaches like Milt Tenopir and Charlie McBride "were a little bit more of yellers," Brown was the coach who never yelled but could lay on a thick guilt trip.

"I looked at him as my dad, so if I did something wrong or didn't perform at the level he expected, he would just kind of put his hands on his hips and look at me funny, and I knew that I felt guilty," Davison said. "I think all of us just played in a way that we didn't want to let our teammates or our coaches down. The level of intensity was high on every play in practice and every play in a game."

Davison calls safety Mike Brown the best teammate, top to bottom, he's ever played with—on the field, off the field, in the locker room, in practice, in games. Brown is also still the best open-field tackler Davison has ever seen play for Nebraska.

Brown's toughness was paralleled, in Davison's eyes, by quarterback Eric Crouch. Davison still recalls a play in which he blocked for Crouch in the 1999 Big 12 Championship game against Texas in San Antonio, a game the Cornhuskers won 22–6.

"He ran up my backside as I was blocking on an option play, and he got hit hard, and we both kind of tumbled to the ground," Davison said. "We gained however many yards and gained a first down, and I jump up and I'm whooping and hollering, and I help Eric up, and as I'm helping him up I notice his chin strap is broken and he has blood coming out of one of the corners of his mouth."

Davison could tell Crouch wasn't right. At the very least, he'd gotten his bell rung.

"We got back to the huddle and I'm waiting for the next play to come in, and I'm like, 'Dude, you got to get your chinstrap fixed,' and he's like, 'I'm fine, I'm fine,' and I just looked at his eyes and was like, 'He's not fine.' I called timeout from the huddle and the coaches were like, 'What are you doing!?' And when Eric got to the sideline they realized he needed like a 60-second break before he could gather himself."

Crouch and Davison were often roommates on road trips, including the Fiesta Bowl game against Tennessee in 2000.

While the team was practicing in Tempe, Arizona, coach Frank Solich received a phone call from Nebraska men's basketball coach Danny Nee, who wondered if Davison had any interest in joining his team that month, after the bowl game, and if Solich would allow it.

Matt Davison is the color commentator for Huskers football and basketball, two sports he played at Nebraska. *(Shelby Tilts of Shelby Suzanne Photography)*

Davison, who'd been playing football for three years, figured he could probably afford to bypass winter conditioning and not miss much, and Solich concurred, giving his permission for Davison to play a couple months of basketball.

It had been more than two years since Davison's intramural basketball team won the campus championship, and he'd not touched a basketball since. So he went to a Phoenix mall and bought one. Back in his hotel room, he'd dribble, lay on his back, toss the ball in the air, and practice his shooting motion. Crouch caught passes.

"We were preparing for the Fiesta Bowl," Davison said, "but I was also getting ready to play basketball."

He picked it back up quicker than he'd anticipated. After only three basketball practices, Davison traveled with the team to No. 8 Kansas. Nee told him he could warm up but that he probably wouldn't play.

"I think it was 2:40 into the game, and our starting two-guard had two fouls, and he put me right in the game," Davison said. "So I was the first guy off the bench, in Allen Fieldhouse, in my first college basketball game, and I guarded Kenny Gregory."

He played 16 minutes and scored two points in his debut, a 97–82 loss to Kansas.

"It was interesting for me to go from such a successful program on campus," Davison said, "where everything was so planned out and executed to perfection, from when you eat to when you meet to when you get your ankles taped to when and how you practice and watch film and all that stuff.

"Everything was just regimented in a perfect way. To go from a program that's number one in the country for a number of years to, on the same campus, another team where there wasn't that level of success…it really gave me perspective on why football was so successful."

Osborne, of course, was the driving force behind that. Davison, though, played only one season under the future Hall of Fame coach. He remembers being in the training room that December day when somebody walked in and said there would be a team meeting in five minutes, with a press conference to follow.

Osborne was retiring.

"He announced it to the team," Davison said. "I just remember everybody in the room crying, a lot of tears. I remember how sad Coach Osborne looked."

Some 180 players slowly filed out of the somber room. Osborne specifically grabbed Davison and Bobby Newcombe, another true freshman who'd made significant contributions, as they exited.

"He has both of us standing there, and I remember him saying to us that he wanted us to know that when he was recruiting us, he didn't know this was going to happen," Davison said, "that he didn't want us to feel like he duped us into coming to Nebraska, thinking we were going to play for him for four or five years, and that really bothered him.

"That is just another great example of his character."

—*Brian Rosenthal*

CHAPTER 18

JERRY MURTAUGH,
SENIOR YEAR

1970

Murtaugh's senior campaign started out just about how every guy would like his year (or day) to start. He was at a photo shoot at the Playboy Mansion in Chicago.

However, he would be in the photos, along with the other Playboy All-Americans for the 1970 season. The all-star team included Ole Miss quarterback Archie Manning and offensive lineman Dan Dierdorf from the University of Michigan.

Murtaugh had a few drinks at Hugh Hefner's home with a fellow Big 8 conference player, Colorado offensive lineman Don Popplewell. They did have a centerfold model with them as their escort for the night at the mansion.

("Nothing happened and I know you were wondering. Signed, J. Murt.")

The party moved to the Playboy Club and Murtaugh was feeling frisky.

"I had a few beers by the time we got to the club," Murtaugh said. "One of the Playboy Bunnies walked by me in her little bunny costume so I pulled her tail."

Unfortunately for Murt there was no Mexican judge to which to give money and switchblades on this misstep.

"All of a sudden two big guys appeared and took me to the door," Murtaugh said. "It was a short night for me at the Playboy Club, so I just went somewhere else and got drunk."

Famously, Murtaugh predicted a national championship before the 1970 season, drawing the ire of Devaney. The season started off with a tough game at USC. While NU outplayed USC, the game ended in a tie.

USC's players did an unusual thing after the game in Los Angeles.

"We were in the locker room and some coaches said the USC captains wanted to talk to us," Murtaugh said. "I thought they might want to fight. But they said, 'Hey you guys out-played us and we just wanted to wish you guys luck.'

"That was a real classy thing they did…after we finished beating on each other."

Jerry Murtaugh (right) after a photo shoot for the Playboy All-Americans at the Playboy Mansion in Chicago with Colorado offensive lineman Don Popplewell and a 1969 Playboy centerfold. *(Courtesy of Jerry Murtaugh)*

NU would go on to win the rest of their games, including a 28–21 victory over Oklahoma in Lincoln, clinching the Big 8 championship. NU needed a fourth-quarter touchdown drive, maybe foreshadowing the Orange Bowl game with the LSU Tigers.

As day went to night on January 1, 1971, No. 3 Nebraska had an outside shot at a national championship because the results of major bowl games were going their way.

No. 1 Texas and No. 2 Ohio State, having lost their games earlier on New Year's Day, gave the Cornhuskers a shot at the program's first national championship. They would face No. 5 LSU, which would have national championship claims as well with a victory in Miami.

With a national championship on the line, NU bolted to a 10–0 lead in the first quarter. But LSU would battle back and lead 12–10 in the

Jerry Murtaugh (right) with his position coach, John Melton, at a late 1990s golf tournament. *(Courtesy of Jerry Murtaugh)*

Orange Bowl to start the fourth quarter.

Quarterback Jerry Tagge would finish a drive with a historic one-yard plunge to give Nebraska the lead. The defense would keep the Tigers from scoring, and NU would win the game and the national championship.

Just like Murtaugh's prediction before the season.

So of course Murtaugh was looking to celebrate and felt the University of Nebraska should foot the bill.

"After the game at the hotel, it cost four or five bucks a beer," Murtaugh said. "And the guys came to me and said we can't afford this, where are we gonna have a party?"

Murtaugh went to Devaney but the coach said he wasn't paying. So Murtaugh decided to hit up another coach for beer money.

"A little bit later I go to Coach Kiffin and ask him, and he says, 'Let me handle it,'" Murtaugh said. "Within an hour he says the room is ready upstairs, there's booze and food and we go up there."

After a few drinks, Murtaugh wanted a few more.

"So we are having a ball and then Eddie [Periard] and I get the same idea to go visit LSU at their hotel and we are pretty drunk," Murtaugh said.

Round 2 with LSU.

"So we go over there and somehow we got in one of their hotel rooms—because when you are drunk you can do anything," Murtaugh said. "The LSU guys are just looking at us and they are pissed."

Of course Murtaugh had something to say.

"I said we just wanted to say hi and good game," Murtaugh said. "I knew we were in a bad spot so I didn't say much more."

The Tigers were upset, but a few of them knew fighting would be a bad option.

"Then the RB and the TE come in, 'Hey we can't do this here,'" Murtaugh said. "And then one of the guys looks at us and says, 'Get the fuck out of here!'"

The Huskers took the advice with some Bayou Bengals following behind them.

"They escort us down the elevator, yelling at us, and we are just walking out," Murtaugh said. "They are watching us walk out the door...and then I turned around and said, 'You motherfuckers, I will kick all your asses!'

"And of course they start coming at us and then we ran back to our hotel laughing the whole way."

All and all, not a surprising cap to Murtaugh's career at Nebraska.

The All-American linebacker would soon hit the All-Star Game circuit after his senior year. His position coach in the 1971 Hula Bowl would be a well-known coach on the East Coast, and he had his own star linebacker with him.

"[Joe] Paterno from Penn State was my coach at the All-Star Game," Murtaugh said. "And he had his little perfect boy Jack Ham with him, who was a hell of a player by the way."

The linebacker from Nebraska and the Penn State coach would not see eye to eye.

"I was doing a drill and he stopped me and said, 'I want you to do it like Jack,'" Murtaugh said.

But Murtaugh told him he was going to do the drill his way, and the coach looked at the Omaha North graduate quizzically.

"Paterno didn't get mad or yell at scream at me…he just gave me an odd look," Murtaugh said.

And Paterno would get the last laugh.

"I must have pissed him off because Paterno started a middle guard over me at linebacker with his boy Jack," Murtaugh said. "Then afterward I was thinking, 'Maybe I should have done it like Jack?'"

Murtaugh did everything well enough, like Jack or not, to get a shot at professional football with the New England Patriots. He would locker next to the biggest name on the team and a fellow rookie.

"Jim Plunkett lockered right next to me," Murtaugh said. "And even though he was a rookie and all the big vets kissed up to him, he said he wanted to hang with us 'nobody' rookies and drink beer with us. We respected that."

Plunkett did show his humor in various ways.

"One day he said, 'Let me see your paycheck,'" Murtaugh said. "I said get out of here. But he kept jabbing at me so I showed my $800 pay-check and he showed me his $10,000 check.

"Then he smiled and said, 'Okay Murt, I'll buy tonight.'"

He could also be a big kid on those outings.

"One night we were drinking beer, and coming back and we saw a tricycle in somebody's yard," Murtaugh said. "So of course Plunkett hops on and he is 6'3", 245 pounds, just cruising down the street."

Until the police came…but they weren't too focused on the law.

"The cop asked for Plunkett's autograph and then suggested to him to maybe put the tricycle back," Murtaugh said.

Two knee injuries in 1971–72 limited Murtaugh to some exhibition games with the Patriots before he retired from pro football. With his "PE degree" in hand he taught some, but eventually worked for Union Pacific from which he retired in Omaha. His son, Ryan, was a linebacker in the Huskers program in the early 1990s but injuries would force him to stop playing at Nebraska.

The athletic director in the early 1990s was Bob Devaney, Murtaugh's old coach and occasional—okay, often—verbal combatant. Murtaugh has never said if Devaney ever looked up Ryan to reminisce about the times he shared with Ryan's dad.

Probably not.

—Jimmy Sheil

CHAPTER 19

JAMIE BURROW

Linebacker, 1997–2001

In the 1980s *Sports Illustrated* had an ad campaign called "GET THE FEELING!" One of the specific ads in the campaign was, *"What's It Feel Like To Find Out You're Just Another High School Hotshot?* GET THE FEELING!" That ad was complete with a photo of a college football player stretching on a field of what seemed like hundreds of players.

The photo was taken in Lincoln, Nebraska, at Memorial Stadium.

In the 1990s, a freshman Huskers linebacker from Iowa, who would end up in his high school's hall of fame, could have starred in an updated version of the ad. The photo would have been shot during fall practice at the hallowed stadium in 1997.

"During one of my first practices it was like cattle getting ready to stampede at me with Aaron Taylor in the front," said Jamie Burrow of the two-time All-American offensive lineman Taylor. "Then they snapped the ball and it seemed the offensive linemen were shot out of a cannon."

The advertisers would have a sequel later in the season with 6'2", 245-pound Cornhusker I-back Dan Alexander traumatizing Burrow this time.

"One time I came through the line untouched on a running play in practice," Burrow said, "and I am thinking I'm gonna make a tackle for a loss on the play. But nope, I about got my arm ripped off from 'Big Dan' just plowing through me."

Burrow took his knocks in 1997 on the scout team and he improved as a player. That was the expectation being the son of a Husker. Burrow's dad, Jimmy, played in the NFL and the CFL after playing at Nebraska in the mid-1970s.

While he was a Husker legacy, Burrow's play on the field at Ames High School made him a scholarship athlete. Burrow was a four-year starter at Ames High, playing linebacker and tight end. He was also a starting forward in basketball and he lettered in track.

Despite this prep resume, he was not sure Nebraska had not made a mistake when it offered him a chance to be a Cornhusker.

"Right after Nebraska [made an offer], I thought 'Did they realize what they just did?'" the 6'1" Burrow said. "I thought I better accept it before they [took] it back."

The coach recruiting him, Dan Young, made an impression.

"I thought Coach Young was hilarious with his dry humor and just a down-to-earth guy. Just goes back to doing things the right way and him and Milt [Tenopir] were just geniuses with the blocking schemes and all these different personalities came together and did something special.

"We all miss Coach Young, [there were] lots of people that cared about him at his funeral."

Burrow did have some other college options, but Husker Jon Hesse was his favorite linebacker in high school. Also the way his dad spoke about the man and type of coach Tom Osborne was made it a relatively easy decision.

Thankfully, a slightly odd recruiting visit did not deter him.

"Jay [Foreman] is a stud and he was my host on my recruiting visit. He takes me, a white boy from Ames, Iowa, to a black fraternity party off-campus and there was like one other white guy there," Burrow said laughing. "It was cool I guess…but I was like, 'Where in the heck are we?'

"I was already committed to Nebraska so maybe they didn't care anyway."

Burrow stayed committed to Nebraska and the work on the scout team the following fall was a wake-up call, but he was not going against Iowa high school teams anymore. The team Burrow was going against would lead the country in rushing on the way to a national championship.

Burrow said it was humbling but he would use it to his advantage. Also, the young linebacker locked on to what he needed to do to get on the field.

"Playing on the scout team was an eye-opener," said Burrow, a middle linebacker. "I knew I needed to get more physical and stronger, and maybe I was a little heavy too."

By spring ball, he made some physical changes—and changes on the field began to happen. All of a sudden a trimmer 240-pound Burrow was not feeling like an overwhelmed football player anymore.

"Just getting in better shape I was fast enough to hold point to carry my guy to the safety for the first time and I thought, 'Okay, I can do this,'" Burrow said.

He would get the chance to show this in 1998. Burrow's first year after his redshirt year would coincide with another person's first year of something in the program. Osborne retired as coach in December 1997 and somebody else would lead NU for the first time since the 1972 season.

The new coach was a familiar face to Burrow, though—Frank Solich, who got bumped up from assistant head coach.

"Frank was animated and could be fiery and would let his emotions out and we appreciated that about him," Burrow said. "But I also appreciated how much taller I was than Frank because I was so much shorter than Tom."

In Solich's first year leading Nebraska, the team was coming off a national championship, the program's third in four years. NU lost the main pieces on both sides of the ball in 1998 with Scott Frost and Ahman Green moving to the NFL on offense. Defensively, the Blackshirts lost Grant Wistrom and Jason Peter line to graduation.

Despite the heavy turnover, Nebraska again won nine games to continue the nine-win streak, which had been going since 1969. NU did lose four games but in those losses all of the games were close. The mentality of competition was still there under Solich, even if they did go from undefeated to four losses. Burrow saw action in 12 games in 1998, mostly on special teams. In limited action, he did have four tackles as he got his first taste of college football.

A strong spring practice in 1999 set the stage for Burrow to be two deep on the depth chart. The next season there was more opportunity, and "little milestones" began to pile up for Burrow. He was part of the group that helped fill the void left by the departures of an All-Big 12 performer in Foreman, plus Eric Johnson. Both linebackers would go on to careers in the NFL.

"My sophomore year from time to time I was able to hang with Dom (Dominic Raiola) and that was a little milestone," Burrow said. "Just learning and applying the concepts so I was playing faster and not thinking as much on the field."

Solich had Nebraska in the national championship picture all season in 1999. Burrow's stats in 1999 increased as he had 14 tackles and a fumble recovery. Burrow mentioned an off-the-field situation possibly helped him channel his energy early that season.

"I broke up with a girl, so maybe I had some pent-up anger," a smiling Burrow said. "Every snap I was just running forward in any direction. Hard. I just wanted to hit people. Maybe I should thank that girl."

Maybe thanking that girl would be a bit unorthodox, but there was someone Burrow could thank. He said he didn't know anything about a Husker coach on defense when he committed to Nebraska, but one coach would become a significant figure in his Huskers career.

"Everyone loves Coach McBride and for good reason," Burrow said. "I didn't know much about Charlie when I committed, but he encompassed everything that Husker football is."

One central thing stood out to Burrow about McBride. The coach preached brotherhood on the team but he also let them know before every game in the locker room that it was not an "us against the world" mentality for Nebraska football.

"Charlie did not talk about you as an individual; he talked about the team, guys playing for each other," Burrow said. "McBride told us there are a lot of people not in this room that you play for. Whether they wore the jersey before you, or your family, the people in the state, and the fans. Just have that in your heart when you take the field."

In McBride's time it was common for players to run into each other trying to get out of the locker room and to the field after his fiery pregame speeches. Also common were some of his sayings in practice.

"Charlie had many funny sayings at practice," Burrow said. "'If it is moving, kill it,' or, 'What do you have pumping through your veins? Kool-aid or the real shit?'

"They were corny but with him it was awesome."

However, Burrow also remembered some of the other comments he received when he made a mistake. But he said these comments were not taken to heart because McBride had developed trust with the players.

They knew when the play was over that was the end of it, and McBride's coaching in practice was going to help them on game day. And McBride was an equal-opportunity hazer, from starters to walk-ons.

"Charlie would yell at me, 'Burrow, when you graduate I will celebrate that day [because] I won't have to look at your face anymore!'" Burrow said, laughing.

In the 1999 season, after what would be their only loss to Texas, the Huskers wanted to see those Longhorn faces again. Burrow would play an unexpectedly bigger role in the rematch versus Texas in the Big 12 Championship in San Antonio.

The Huskers were out for revenge after blowing a 10-point halftime lead during the regular season in Austin. Burrow mentioned the close calls that seemed to all go Texas' way in that Big 12 road game.

Husker fans will not soon forget Texas defensive lineman Casey Hampton recovering a fumble out of bounds and Texas getting possession. Or Nebraska safety Mike Brown getting his jersey almost ripped off on a Longhorn touchdown in the fourth quarter with no penalty.

"We were so happy to play Texas in the Big 12 championship. We felt we got robbed earlier in the season," Burrow said. "Maybe the refs just blew the calls, but we wanted that rematch bad."

In the Big 12 championship an early-game injury to starting middle linebacker Carlos Polk opened the door for Burrow to get some significant playing time. Also, Nebraska would tweak its game plan a bit and they would need aggressive play from the middle linebacker.

In that prior matchup, Texas staged a second-half comeback as NU was not overly aggressive with blitzes late in the game and Texas capitalized on that to make plays. It wasn't a bad ploy since Texas only had three points at halftime of their regular season game.

However, in the rematch, McBride vowed that would not happen again, and Burrow would find himself as the tip of the spear on blitzes. NU would take control of the game in the second quarter on both sides of the ball.

Burrow was part of many disruptive plays and hit Longhorn quarterback Major Applewhite repeatedly as NU raced to 22–0 third-quarter lead. The Huskers coasted to a 22–6 win in a game that was never in doubt. Burrow totaled two quarterback hurries, one tackle for loss on Applewhite, one pass breakup, and two tackles as a non-starter.

On the plane ride home, Burrow wanted to party for more than the recently won hardware—as he had just turned 21 years old. The Big 12 champ and 21-year-old announced on the plane home that there would be a party at his place. He went right to a liquor store to stock up, but he got an unexpected surprise.

"While I am buying the first keg of my life," Burrow said, "ESPN was playing highlights. In the checkout line I am hearing my name called—a surreal experience—[my] first time on ESPN and buying a keg.

"Not a bad day for a college kid."

After destroying Texas, the Huskers were set for a matchup with the Tennessee Volunteers in the Fiesta Bowl. Unfortunately, the earlier Texas loss kept Nebraska from playing for the national championship. Many felt NU was best-suited to face undefeated Florida State, but Virginia Tech got the nod with its undefeated record.

In the Fiesta Bowl, Nebraska raced to a 17–0 lead in the second quarter but the Volunteers closed it to 17–14 in the third quarter. Then Nebraska imposed its will and went up 31–14. Tennessee did score a touchdown in the fourth quarter but NU held the ball for the last seven minutes of the game by rushing on 13 consecutive plays and taking a knee deep in Volunteer territory as time expired.

For the game, NU rushed for 321 yards and "Big Dan" harassed Tennessee defenders with 108 yards on 21 carries. Tennessee rushed for only 44 yards, which played into Nebraska controlling the ball for 34 minutes of the game to Tennessee's 26 minutes.

Two senior Huskers who had big days in the Fiesta Bowl were safety Mike Brown and defensive tackle Steve Warren. Brown finished with seven tackles, a pass break-up, and an interception en route to earning Defensive MVP honors. Warren posted his seventh game of the 1999 season with two or more tackles for loss, finishing with three tackles, including two for loss.

Both Blackshirts would make the All-American team and Burrow had a front-row seat for their unique skill sets.

"Woo [Warren] was a 320-pound ballerina," Burrow said. "A play would start and I knew where I was supposed to end up and many times I thought I was going to run into him. But Woo would do a Tim Hardaway spin move and be right where he was supposed to be and make the play. That is why he was an All-American and he played in the NFL."

While Warren was in front of Burrow, Brown was behind him on the Blackshirt defense. Burrow mentioned it wasn't only Brown's physical ability that amazed him.

"My guy Mike had tons of passion and heart," Burrow said. "But some don't realize just how good his instincts were.

"I remember watching game film during the week and it was amazing week after week. At the snap of the ball the rest of the defense was going one way and he would go the other and the play would end up right where Mike was going. He just saw things nobody else did."

The last two games put an exclamation point on the 1999 season, which would lead to a high ranking to start the 2000 season. Also, big games on the schedule included playing at Notre Dame and at Oklahoma.

In 2000, being an upperclassman at Nebraska, Burrow's day-to-day life got a little easier.

"We had some hazing that has since been ruled illegal probably," Burrow said with a smile. "When you graduated into the varsity locker room, you had to pay rent."

However, this would not involve money.

"Paying rent was getting pseudo-beat-up with Wiffle ball bats," Burrow said. "Your name might be on the wall and they would bring you in one at a time and you would get swatted a bit. But it was never as bad as the older guys would make it seem. Probably like a frat."

Burrow's junior year saw him play behind the All-American candidate in Polk who rarely left the field. However, Burrow wound up finishing the season with 14 tackles after his first career sack. For the team, a fast start with a big road win over Notre Dame was upended by a few Big 12 losses to Oklahoma and Kansas State on the road. NU did finish strong by pummeling Northwestern in the Alamo Bowl 66–17.

For Burrow's senior season in 2001, he was set to start on a team with a Heisman candidate in quarterback Eric Crouch. Burrow had seen Crouch as much as anyone since they came in together in 1997 and the physical quarterback was one of a kind according to Burrow.

"Eric was a warrior and would do whatever you needed him to do," Burrow said. "And he was always playing injured, just a physical player but he [had] some shake too."

Some days Crouch made you look worse than others.

"One day in Cook Pavilion in the open field, he shook me bad," Burrow said. "We both planted and I thought I had him. And he went the other way and maybe it caused me to have a back spasm. It looked like a sniper got me and I just fell down without touching him and he ran by.

"It was embarrassing as they dragged me to the sideline and then to the training room."

Even when Burrow had a good game, he was talking about Crouch.

"After the Mizzou game my senior year, I was starting to get more attention so I was getting interviewed after we beat them," Burrow said. "I remember shifting the interview to Eric. I said, 'The things Eric can do to a defender are sick and wrong.'"

Burrow was speaking from experience. In this case, he was talking about Crouch's 95-yard touchdown run out of a pass play that broke down. Crouch ran maybe 120 yards on that touchdown jaunt in Columbia, Missouri.

In the non-conference season in 2001, Burrow showed he was ready to uphold the Blackshirt tradition at Nebraska. In a highly anticipated Notre Dame game in Lincoln, he had 11 tackles in the game that was basically over at halftime with Nebraska up 27–3. His performance garnered him the Defensive Player of the Week honors for the Big 12 conference. His coach was not shocked.

"The honor is really well deserved," Solich said to sportswriter John Gaskins after the game. "There was a belief that Jamie would have a great year because every time he got opportunities, he showed it. And it was great to see it all come together for us in the game against Notre Dame."

The Sooners would be a bigger challenge than the Fighting Irish later in the season, with both teams coming in undefeated.

Coming into the late-season game Oklahoma was ranked No. 1 or No. 2 in the country, depending on the poll, and Nebraska was ranked third in the nation. Nebraska would knock off Oklahoma in a game that would be remembered for a late-game Husker trick play called "Black 41 Flash Reverse Pass." The pass from receiver Mike Stunz to Crouch would put the game away and the Huskers won 20–10.

While Burrow was again the Big 12 Defensive Player of the Week with double-digit tackles and this time the Bronko Nagurski National

Player of the Week as well, the game did not start out well for Burrow. And a coach on the Husker sideline let him know about it.

"My dad was a grad assistant at the time on the team," Burrow said. "On the first series the Sooners did a jet sweep and I missed a tackle on the Oklahoma guy. I came off the field and my dad got in my face and said, 'Make a damn tackle!'"

The way Burrow figured it, it was a double whammy.

"It was bad enough having a coach tell you that, but your dad, too," Burrow said, laughing. "Also, I had lots of relatives at the game and they had great seats and probably saw my dad getting on me as well."

Burrow would heed those words from his dad as the game wore on. Burrow would end the game with 17 tackles. The win put Nebraska in the driver's seat for the national championship, and Burrow let the nation know who they just took down.

"After the game in the press conference, I could not resist having a little fun," Burrow said. "I said, 'Any time you play the No. 1 team in the country—I mean, former number one team in the country....'"

In 2001, on the national championship hunt, Burrow's understudy was true freshman Barrett Ruud. The young linebacker would go on to finish his career as the all-time leader in tackles at Nebraska and end up with 432 total tackles as a Husker. He would also play in the NFL for eight seasons, mostly with the Tampa Bay Buccaneers.

Some of those 432 tackles Ruud made cost more than others. Kansas State I-back Joe Hall weighed close to 330 pounds and fifth-year senior Burrow had a plan as they prepared for the Wildcats in a late-season game in 2001.

"Joe Hall was a monster and I was not gonna mess around with him. He was a 300-pound running back," Burrow said. "Before the game I just decided I would take his legs out—less energy and probably better results."

However, the linebacker's protégé had other ideas. Ruud would be in store for the *"How Does It Feel To Know You're Just Another High School Hotshot?"* feeling Burrow had as a freshman.

"But Barrett, the young buck, was gonna take on Hall," Burrow said. "So Hall gets past the line of scrimmage and Barrett goes high on him. He ended up jumping on Hall's back and it was like he was a human backpack and he got carried maybe 15 yards with T.J. Hollowell getting left in the wreckage."

A review of the stats from that Husker 31–21 win over Kansas State showed Burrow with 13 total tackles and Ruud with two. Hopefully the other one was not as adventurous.

After beating Kansas State and later Kansas, NU was on track for the Big 12 title and a possible national championship.

But then the game at Colorado happened.

Two games earlier, in a win over Kansas, safety Phil Bland was lost for the season with an injury. The Cornhuskers defense took a hit with Bland's loss but Nebraska was still favored in the game at Colorado. Those elements contributed to a perfect storm of events that led to a shocking 62–36 Buff win.

However, another perfect storm of events occurred with every team ahead of Nebraska losing, and the Cornhuskers found themselves in the national championship game in the Rose Bowl, despite the Colorado loss and not even playing in the Big 12 championship game. Nebraska would face Miami, a team full of All-Big East players who would go on to the NFL as well. The Hurricanes won handily 37–14 after jumping out to a 34–0 lead in Pasadena, California.

Burrow would make the All-Big 12 team, after leading the Huskers in tackles with 84, and have a shot at the NFL. Burrow spent time with the New York Jets organization before retiring, leaving time to watch his younger brothers play college football.

In fact, one of the younger brothers was a teammate. In 2001, Dan Burrow was a redshirt freshman and a reserve safety. Dan finished his career in 2004 with the nickname "The Pebble" to Jamie's nickname of "The Rock."

His youngest brother, Joe, signed a letter of intent in 2015 to play football at Ohio State as a quarterback. There is a decent chance Joe will face his dad and brothers' team in the near future. If so, Jamie would likely be at the stadium, but there is a chance he might have to watch the Husker-Buckeye game from his work.

Big brother Jamie owns a Louie's Wine Dive franchise in Omaha, and Husker football games can be a standing-room-only event at his restaurant. The casual and upscale eatery features unique dishes and hard-to-find wines.

Maybe Burrow should dedicate a dish, or a drink, at his restaurant to his older teammates Aaron Taylor or "Big Dan" Alexander since they helped prepare him for a memorable and all-conference career as a Cornhusker?

—*Jimmy Sheil*

CHAPTER 20

ADAM CARRIKER

Defensive End, 2002–06

Adam Carriker won't soon forget what he calls the two hardest, most physically grueling weeks of his life.

He won't forget the reason behind them, either, or how it inspired and motivated him during his time with the Nebraska Cornhuskers and his ensuing career in the NFL.

New head coach Bill Callahan, less than a year removed from leading the Oakland Raiders to Super Bowl XXXVII, was bringing his NFL mentality to Lincoln, and that meant there was no need for 180 players on the roster. So he designed what Carriker described as "two weeks of hell," a period between winter conditioning and spring practice of 2004, in what was the beginning of the ill-fated Callahan regime.

"Basically," Carriker said, "the design was to get guys to quit."

The sessions began at 4:00 AM. That meant getting taped at 3:30 AM. That meant waking up at 3:00 AM. For two straight weeks.

"Each coach had a station, and every station was basically insanity, from a 225-sled pull to doing up-downs for five straight minutes to doing ropes nonstop," Carriker said. "There was one station where they gave you a break. You got on your knees and acted like you were thrusting, out hitting somebody. It was basically a reason to give you a break. Other than that, every station was insanity.

"We would do four gassers at the end of this, then four-and-a-half, then five, and it was the most insane conditioning I ever did in my life. There were guys puking, guys keeled over."

Each day, fewer and fewer players, the majority of them walk-ons, were showing up. Callahan's plan was working. By the time spring practice began, the roster was closer to 120 players.

More attrition occurred after the 2004 season, when Nebraska finished 5–6 and missed a bowl game for the first time in over 40 years. Cornerback Fabian Washington and safety Josh Bullocks left early for the NFL. Quarterback Joe Dailey and wide receiver Ross Pilkington were captains and only sophomores but they left the program, too.

"It was really bad for a lot of guys for a long time," Carriker said. "That's why a lot of guys left. It was hard for me to stick it out, but I did. This was my lifelong dream. I wasn't going to give it away. I had to find other reasons to play."

How big of a dream was Nebraska for Carriker, who grew up in Washington but had Nebraska roots?

Well, had you asked Carriker during his junior year of high school to list his top three colleges, he wouldn't have put Nebraska on the list—not because he didn't want to play for the Cornhuskers, but because the mere thought of going there seemed such a far-fetched impossibility, he wouldn't have thought to name them.

"To me, I didn't care how bad it got, how dark it got," Carriker said. "I loved that place so much I was going to stay."

Born in Hastings, Nebraska, Carriker was three years old when his family moved to Washington. His father grew up on a small farm near Giltner, Nebraska, and instilled his love of Husker football into his sons.

"My mom makes fun of him because back in the '70s, '80s, when they played Oklahoma on Thanksgiving Day, he'd be trembling before the game, he'd be so nervous," Carriker said. "That's the kind of environment [in which] I was raised up in the state of Washington."

Carriker's high school football teams weren't good. They won two games in four years, making it somewhat difficult for college teams to gauge his talent level. He'd received letters from various schools but had narrowed his list to the four major ones in the Great Northwest: Oregon, Oregon State, Washington, and Washington State. And Nebraska, which hadn't offered a scholarship.

The Huskers did offer a gray shirt, or the invitation to play as a walk-on for one season with the assumption of a scholarship to follow. But Carriker wouldn't be able to afford tuition and decided he'd need a scholarship to attend college. He called and told Nebraska coaches Frank Solich, George Darlington, and Nelson Barnes that he'd be choosing either Washington State or Oregon State (Oregon had pulled its offer) because it was monetarily more feasible.

"It wasn't even a full day later," Carriker said. "Nebraska calls and offers me a full scholarship after we had said 'no' to the gray shirt. I'm not going to lie, it kind of twarked me off a little bit. Clearly you wanted me; you were just trying to get me to go to Nebraska on a gray shirt."

Upset, Carriker didn't give a response immediately. He took his recruiting visit to Oregon State, where he'd been "a ton of times," and also visited Washington State before finally taking a trip to Lincoln.

"While I was there, I remember talking to my dad, going, 'I want to go here, it's my dream school, it still is. I'm just still a little bit upset about [the gray shirt].'

"He goes, 'Well, I think it's time for you to get over that if this is where you want to go.' So I did. I went up to Solich's office and I committed."

When Carriker first arrived on campus, players on the scout team weren't treated the greatest. Hazing was prominent. Players, at that time, were divided into two locker rooms—the south locker room for veterans and the north locker room for newcomers and walk-ons.

"If you were a young guy, you didn't go by the south locker room," Carriker said. "Not that they would beat you to a bloody pulp or anything like that, but they would have fun with you, and a lot of times you wouldn't feel that good afterward. You just knew not to walk by the south locker room."

One hazing practice was called 'paying the rent,' which Callahan eliminated, as he did most practices other than haircuts. "The idea was you lay down in the middle of the room and they had Wiffle ball bats and they'd pour Gatorade on you and they had paddles they'd hit you in the rear end with," Carriker said.

One of the ringleaders was offensive lineman Richie Incognito, an instigator both in the locker room and on the field.

Adam Carriker with his wife, Angie, and children, Addison and Jacob, before a Washington Redskins game. *(Courtesy of Adam Carriker)*

"I watched him get into a fight with every single defensive lineman at some point, and nine of the 11 starters overall, linebackers and DBs. He didn't care how big or small you were. He didn't care," Carriker said.

"The next year, I was starting, I was going against him every day. I'm hitting him every play. We're eventually going to get into a fight. It's an impossibility that it's not going to happen. Then it was interesting. They actually moved Richie to center, and I was like, 'Okay, I guess I'm not going to have to worry about that.'"

Except that one day, in fall camp, coaches had a goal-line segment in practice, and nose guard LeKevin Smith was out. Coaches inserted Carriker in his place, pitting him against Incognito.

"I went against Richie, knocked him back about 5 yards, and he didn't like that," Carriker said. "He starts swinging. I'd seen him fight a million times. He'd probably never seen me fight. So I knew exactly what he was going to do. I've always said it's like I had the film and he didn't. But he chose to make it that way.

"He started swinging. I started swinging as well. More of my punches landed."

Ironically, the player Carriker ended up going against more than anybody else in his entire career was Incognito—three straight years at Nebraska, and then three more years when the players were together on the St. Louis Rams.

"He was first team All-Big 12 that previous year, and I had just got to Nebraska, so I was going against him every day in practice, and I was doing very well," Carriker said. "I was actually winning a lot more one-on-one battles than I was losing. To me, that was kind of like, 'Okay, I can do this, I can play here,' because he was very good, despite his reputation. He can play football, and I was more than holding my own against him."

But Incognito's aggression eventually led to his dismissal from the Nebraska program by Callahan in 2004. The last straw, Carriker said, was a memorable locker room fight between Incognito and wide receiver Grant Mulkey.

"I was sitting in the cold tub icing my ankle, and I could see through the glass, and all of a sudden I see Richie just take off after Grant," Carriker said. "Everyone separates them, they're yelling at each other and then Richie goes after him again, they separate him…I can't hear anything. I can just see it all through the glass.

"The ironic thing was Grant and Richie were like best friends. They hung out all the time. It's a good thing they separated Grant and Richie, because Grant, he was like 180 pounds. That wouldn't have gone well."

That was another dark spot in a 2004 season that Carriker, then a sophomore, recalls as the worst year of football he had in his life. The low point was a 70–10 loss at Texas Tech, the worst in program history, and Carriker remembers Texas Tech fans making an 'L' shape with their hands on their foreheads.

Or so he thought. He later found out that fans were actually making the traditional "Guns up" signal, usually whenever the Red Raiders did something good, which, on that night, was quite frequent.

"The whole night I'm thinking, 'These people are stupid. Why are they giving us the elementary sign for 'loser' on their foreheads?'" Carriker said. "The joke was on me, as it turned out."

Carriker felt bad for the seniors that season, especially Jeff McBride, the brother of Carriker's girlfriend, Angie, and now his brother-in-law.

The final game of that season, at home against Colorado, coaches had moved the 240-pound McBride, a walk-on, from defensive end to defensive tackle because the team was terribly thin at the position. Brandon Teamer, a true freshman playing as a backup, was injured, leaving Nebraska with its two starters and McBride.

"There were times during that year you could tell he wanted nothing to do with football, but in that game, I've never been so proud of an individual," Carriker said. "A guy from a small town, a walk-on, who'd never played any snaps that had counted, playing 240 pounds at D-tackle, and he spelled those two starters and he played well. I watched the film later, and he didn't have a bad snap the entire game.

"I've never actually told him because it would be awkward, but I've never been more proud of a football player in my life than when I watched him that game."

The next two seasons were a little brighter for Carriker. In 2005, his junior season, Nebraska was seemingly gaining momentum with a three-game winning streak to close the season. That included a stirring victory in the Alamo Bowl against a Michigan team that had begun the season highly ranked and boasted a bevy of future NFL players.

"Going into that game, their left tackle was like two-time All-Big Ten, I had a really good year as a junior, so the whole to-do was me versus this left tackle," Carriker said. "The first two plays of the game I threw him on his face. The third play, I go over to the other side [of the line], and I go against some sophomore I'd never heard of, and he locks me up. I can't get away from him.

"I come over to the sideline, I go, 'Coach, are you sure the All-Big Ten guy's not the right tackle?' He goes, 'No, he's on the left side.' I killed the All-Big Ten guy the whole game. Then the guy on the right side, we were going back and forth. He would get me, I would get him."

The player on the right side, then only a sophomore, was Jake Long, who would be the No. 1 pick of the 2008 NFL Draft.

In Carriker's senior season, Nebraska mounted a late comeback at Texas A&M, with Maurice Purify hauling in a game-winning touchdown pass from Zac Taylor in the final seconds that clinched a Big 12 North Division title. Carriker had a sack to end that game, which he was thankful was finally over, for several reasons.

"I remember during the game, I couldn't look up in the stands," he said. "Only time in my life I couldn't look in the stands, because they do that thing where they sway back and forth, and I [would get] dizzy.

Adam Carriker with pro wrestler John Cena, a former college football player, in 2012. Carriker is an avid wrestling fan and may end up in the ring someday. *(Courtesy of Adam Carriker)*

Every time I'd look in the stands I'd get dizzy and have to throw up. So I had to stare down at the field the whole time."

Carriker, through conversations with those who knew Callahan, surmised that Callahan was still upset about being fired from the Raiders and took out his frustrations on his first Nebraska team. Hence his lack of understanding or caring for many Nebraska traditions, like the walk-on program.

219

But Callahan did help increase the talent level in his four seasons at Nebraska. He did so with the help of assistant coach John Blake, who became Carriker's favorite coach. While not necessarily the most organized coach, Blake's relationship with players was strong and genuine.

"He approached it as 'I legitimately care about you as a human being, you can come talk to me anytime, anywhere, anything you need, I'm here for you, I'll do it for you,'" Carriker said. "It was part of the reason he was such a great recruiter. There were some people who acted that way when they recruited guys, and then when they got there, they could treat them completely differently.

"Coach Blake wasn't that way. He would actually be more so that way, especially if you were one of his guys. He made football about passion. He made it about the love of the game and playing hard and having fun."

Carriker witnessed his share of impressive individual performances from teammates while at Nebraska. He'd never seen a defensive tackle with a spin move like Titus Adams.

"He had pigeon feet. His toes almost touched when he ran. He would lose one-on-one pass rushes just to set up a spin move, and then when he busted it out, he would make offensive linemen look silly," Carriker said.

"The most impressive thing I ever saw him do, [was a] half fake spin one direction and then he would spin completely back the other way. It was like a guy in a slam-dunk competition but without the basketball and the hoops. His spin move was insane."

Carriker remembers one day in the weight room with nose guard Ryon Bingham when they were instructed to do high repetitions.

"He goes up to me and says, 'How do I put 275 on the bar?' and I'm looking at him like, 'What?' And he goes, 'I never lift below 315. I always warm up with 315.' I looked at him like, 'Are you freaking kidding me?'

"He made it look like a feather. I never saw him lift with anything less than 315 after that, ever. I always paid attention to it. I've never ever heard of that anywhere else, NFL or otherwise."

Carriker earned his first Blackshirt his sophomore year and still has three of them. The original one he has framed in his basement. He gave one to his girlfriend and now wife, Angie, and the other to his parents.

"I'll never forget the day I got my Blackshirt. That was a pretty cool day," Carriker said. "You would come in and it would be hung up in your locker, so you would know before you went to meetings who got their Blackshirts. Then we'd go to the meetings and they'd play a video, a short clip of each guy who got their Blackshirt, maybe 10 seconds per guy.

"That was about one of the coolest days of my life, because a Blackshirt is such a unique tradition, and it's something I always looked up to my entire life. I thought that was pretty freaking cool."

No matter if Nebraska was playing Nichols State or Texas or Oklahoma, Carriker would get emotional to the point of tears before every home game, especially during the famed Tunnel Walk, realizing his childhood dream had come true. "It's weird," he said. "It's like a movie in my mind."

On Senior Day, Carriker was proud to have his father walk on the field for the first time during a game and see Memorial Stadium on game day from a different perspective.

"He was the reason Nebraska was my dream and he was the person who believed in me, even in times when it didn't look like things were going to go my way," Carriker said.

"I was kind of a wild card because my team wasn't great, so it was kind of hard to judge me when there were other guys coming in who were more highly recruited. My goal was just to go to Nebraska and not get my butt kicked, if you want to know the honest truth. I went from a guy who came here and just didn't want to get pancaked to a guy who earned being a captain."

—Brian Rosenthal

CHAPTER 21

ZAC TAYLOR

Quarterback, 2005–06

In Oklahoma, football is a religion and despite setting records at Norman High School, Zac Taylor was not heavily recruited in state.

Even being a legacy to the Oklahoma Sooners—his father, Sherman, was a Sooner defensive back, captain of the team, and a graduate assistant coach—Zac was passed up as an option. Instead, Zac attended Wake Forest, where he redshirted before he transferred to Butler Community College in Kansas. There he passed for nearly 3,000 yards and threw 29 touchdowns, and caught the eye of University of Nebraska head coach Bill Callahan.

Callahan was abandoning Nebraska's longstanding option offense and running game to implement the West Coast offense. He needed a compact passer, and Zac fit the bill. So in 2005, with one last momentous school transfer, Zac became a Cornhusker.

While abandoning tradition and the running game in Nebraska was sacrilege to many, Zac saw it as a challenge. Zac's focus was on having to adjust to a new school, new classes, and new friends so the pressure to perform, against tradition, wasn't his main concern. This was Zac's third school. He just wanted to play and play well. He knew why he was there, and he wanted to win.

The weather proved to be tough to navigate. Zac recalls his first day of class in January. It was zero degrees, and he was not prepared for the cold. He had no clue how to navigate the campus or Lincoln, Nebraska. The streets in Lincoln are lettered in alphabetical order, and Zac had trouble reading the map to his classes. He was supposed to be on 'P' Street but he was on 'O' Street. As a result, Zac spent two hours in the frigid cold, stopping into bars and restaurants to ask for directions without the right winter gear for a cold Nebraska day.

Freezing, Zac gave up suffering in the cold and missed the first day of class completely. With the first day of school behind him, Zac was ready to play football.

Entering the 2005 season, Zac was a complete stranger to the

Cornhuskers. "I really didn't know what to expect or what was going to happen," he told the *Omaha World-Herald*. "I didn't know if I'd be the worst quarterback in the country, or even starting, for that matter." Spring practice was a four-way battle that included incumbent Joe Dailey. Zac won the starting job by throwing for three touchdowns in the spring game.

Zac's Husker career began to accelerate, albeit slowly at first until the fourth game against Iowa State. Taylor had a break-out game, illuminating his talents with two touchdowns, 431 passing yards, and a 65.5 completion percentage.

From there he continued to improve, breaking the school passing record of 2,653 yards. He began to show his true talents, the ones that Callahan saw and invested in. One game Zac is extremely proud of was the final game of his junior year. Zac and the Huskers beat rival Colorado 30–3, dominating in every way.

Zac recalls watching Colorado play football every Thanksgiving Day glued to the TV. Colorado became one of Zac's favorite teams to play and this first game turned out to be epic as the Huskers slew their rival on their home turf. The win took Colorado out of contention and solidified Nebraska's position in the Big 12 Championship. The Huskers would beat Colorado both years that Zac was at the helm.

This was a true coming-out game for many Husker players, especially Zac as starting quarterback, and for the team's new West Coast offense. The Huskers ended the winning season with a trip to the Alamo Bowl. In one of the most bizarre endings in a bowl game, No. 20 Michigan deployed a trick play and passed the ball nine times but fumbled the ball in the end zone. Michigan thought its ball carrier was down for a touchdown. Nebraska was calling for a fumble. Players and coaches all hit the field, and it was unclear who the winner was. Officials voted, giving Zac and the Huskers a bowl win defeating Michigan 32–28.

In 2006—Zac's senior year—on Preseason Media Day, Zac said he, Coach Callahan, and the entire Husker team came in with one goal:

the Big 12 Championship. Zac said, "That's why you go to a school like Nebraska. You want to go to the championships!" The coaches all knew they had talented individual players. But they had something else: drive. Zac was honored to be a team captain with the opportunity to lead the Huskers to another winning season, and he would deliver.

While battling his way back to the Big 12 Championship, Zac had another monumental game against Texas A&M. A late-game interception by the Aggies seemed to seal a Husker defeat in the back-and-forth battle. But Zac threw a 9-yard touchdown to Maurice Purify with seconds left to earn the win with a final score of 28–27. The nail-biter solidified another Husker trip to the Big 12 Championship. The team had achieved their goal set before the season began—they were championship bound.

The Huskers, however, saw defeat in the Battle of the Big Reds. Oklahoma, the Big 12 South division winner, beat Nebraska, the Big 12 North division winner, 21–7. Zac expresses deep disappointment in his own performance, admitting that he "played terrible." He praises the defense for holding Oklahoma down in points, but Zac says his interceptions cost the team the game.

"It is difficult to work so hard for something all year and not deliver," Taylor said.

While Zac felt a personal defeat for the Big 12 loss, which cost the Huskers a trip to the Fiesta Bowl, he did lead the team to the Cotton Bowl and a 9–5 winning season. Zac was named Big 12 Offensive Player of the Year.

Zac attributes his career success to excellent coaching at Nebraska. The coaches worked him hard, pushing his abilities to make him better. Quarterbacks coach Jay Norvell was a tough critic, but he was also good with the praise. Zac has tremendous respect for Coach Norvell and his wife, who would call Zac after every game to check in. Dave Kennedy, strength coach, helped Zac with his physical and mental preparedness. The two would later work together at Texas A&M.

Zac Taylor and his wife, Sarah, in 2014. Taylor was All-Big 12 in 2006 for the Cornhuskers. *(Courtesy of Zac Taylor)*

Zac credits Callahan with prepping him and giving him wisdom. Zac would use these lessons to become a successful coach himself. When promoting Taylor for All-Big 12 honors, Callahan said the quarterback single-handedly made the West Coast offense the norm at Nebraska, which won or shared three national championships in the 1990s with a bruising, run-oriented offense.

"He's flourished. On top of everything else, he just competes like crazy," Callahan said. "He's a tough competitor; he is relentless. He's a guy you want behind the controls."

Zac's father has also clearly been a model for his success.

In a recent article with an Oklahoma reporter, Zac revealed how

Sherwood Taylor emphasized to his sons that life is about building relationships with those who are part of every facet of your life. Those relationships can allow you to build networks and contacts that are invaluable as you grind through life.

"I preached to them, 'It's your contacts," Sherwood Taylor advised the local reporter. "It's everything. You can be the smartest thing in the world, but if you don't get the opportunity...."

With Zac's Nebraska pedigree and contacts, doors have opened for him. Taylor is now the Miami Dolphins' quarterbacks coach. Opportunity has been abundant for the Taylor brothers. Press Taylor is an offensive quality control coach for the Philadelphia Eagles. "It's awesome," Zac Taylor said. "It's a rare experience that two brothers get to share. You're always proud of your brother when something great happens to him."

Those who do not know better might assume Zac married his way into the NFL. Mike Sherman, who was head coach at Texas A&M and was the Dolphins' offensive coordinator from 2012 to 2013, is his father-in-law. Sherman retained Zac at his two most recent stops at A&M and Miami.

Zac doesn't resent or cry foul at the suggestions regarding his relationship with Sherman. "I certainly owe a lot of my experiences to him," Taylor said. "I played quarterback my whole career. There's always skepticism.

"You have to learn to make it work. You're at work [together] every day all day. We definitely have a great relationship. We've made it work.

"I've been fortunate. I've learned a lot from him."

Sherwood Taylor was a coach, too—he was an All-State player at Ada, started at safety for Barry Switzer's teams in the late 1970s, and then coached at both Kansas State and Oklahoma in the 1980s.

Zac's love of football flows much deeper than his relationship with his father-in-law. It came from his father

"He was such a great teacher, it was natural to learn from him [and] be inspired by him," Zac said.

"Great kid, great family," Norvell said. "Football family. Absolutely love that kid and knew he would be an excellent coach from the day I met him and recruited him.

"His makeup is why we recruited him up there. Sharp football mind."

While the coaches influenced Zac as a Husker and beyond, it was his teammates who directly aided in Zac's success. Zac said defensive end Adam Carriker was one of the best leaders and mentors.

"Carriker was always prepared, a complete motivator, and a very hard hitter." According to Zac, Carriker never took it easy on him, making him a better player.

As tough as Carriker was, Zac said the toughest player on the team was fullback Dane Todd. Zac explains that there was a lot of tradition in his position, and if Todd would get a stinger on a play he would refuse to come out of the game. To Zac, friend and backup quarterback Joe Ganz was a different kind of tough. Zac explains that during travel, the team was required to wear sports coats. Ganz would rib Taylor relentlessly, saying his sports jacket made him look like a high school history teacher. During an interview, when asked who the worst-dressed member of the team was, Ganz gave up Zac's name and his history-teacher style. The news got back to Zac's mother, who believed her boy was being teased and shunned by his teammates, and she feared that Zac had no friends. What was a mother to do? Send a check for $400 for him to buy a new jacket, of course.

Today, Zac has no problem buying his own clothes. He has entered his fourth season as a quarterbacks coach for the Miami Dolphins. Before that, he was the assistant coach at Texas A&M. Zac says he is in it for the long haul, coaching football for as long as he can.

Zac's time at Nebraska, while only two seasons, are as accomplished as any quarterback in Nebraska history. Among his feats:

• 2006 Big 12 Offensive Player of the Year (Associated Press,

Coaches, *Kansas City Star, Houston Chronicle, Austin American-Statesman, Dallas Morning News, Fort Worth Star-Telegram*)
- 2006 First-Team All-Big 12 (AP, Coaches, *Kansas City Star, Houston Chronicle, Austin American-Statesman, Dallas Morning News, Fort Worth Star-Telegram*)
- 2006 Nebraska Offensive MVP
- 2006 Guy Chamberlin Trophy Winner
- 2006 Davey O'Brien Award, Manning Award, Maxwell Award Watch Lists
- 2006 Second-Team Academic All-Big 12
- Nebraska Season Record Holder for Touchdowns (26; 2006), and Attempts (430; 2005)
- Nebraska Single-Game Record Holder for Completions (36), and Yards per Completion (26.33)
- 2006 Big 12 Commissioner's Spring Academic Honor Roll
- 2006 Big 12 Commissioner's Fall Academic Honor Roll
- 2006 Brook Berringer Citizenship Team

Zac is married to Sarah, who worked at Nebraska University in sports information when they met. Together they have two sons. Thinking of his own small boys, Zac remembers growing up in Norman as a kid and looking up to the Oklahoma players, especially the quarterbacks. He now translates that memory into his professional career, attempting to be a positive role model for other young kids who now might look up to him.

Zac still loves to see the Nebraska faithful sporting their Cornhuskers gear all over the country. He said, "Nebraska has fan support like no other!" Zac said the one thing he would have done differently in his time at Nebraska would have been to travel more. He only spent two years in Lincoln and he says he would like to hit the coffee shops, see the farmers on their tractors, and talk to the many great fans in Nebraska.

Taylor came into the program at a time when there was a tremendous amount of uncertainty about the future path of Nebraska football. The culture was clearly changing. The Devaney legacy line had officially been terminated. Turmoil was abundant, and dissension was deep. Taylor, it can be said, did more than any single player has done to hold the Husker nation together. While he may not be remembered with the reverence Nebraska has for Jerry Tagge, Turner Gill, Tommie Frazier, or Scott Frost, Zac's record clearly indicates that he deserves to be more than a footnote in the annals of Nebraska football history.

—George Achola

CHAPTER 22

MIKE CAPUTO

Offensive Lineman, 2007–11

Mike Caputo looks the part. He sits in his new office in an orange company polo and khakis. A set of golf clubs sits in the corner of the office and his desk is strewn with product books the size of his old Nebraska playbooks. However, the information is no longer about blocking schemes and pass protections, but details on the new Range Rovers coming to market soon.

Caputo is broad and still in football shape, and the arm tattoos peering out from under his shirt beg to tell the story. He has now come back home, back to the family business at Markel BMW in Omaha—and back to the comfort that helped shape his career in football.

At barely 6'1" and usually well under 300 pounds, Caputo is often written about as an undersized center. He downplays that fact, but it has been an integral part of both his tremendous success and his ceiling in a game that is ever reliant on bigger and taller, right or wrong.

He came to Nebraska as a walk-on in 2007, although he was a Husker long before that. He recalls the moment that Nebraska football permeated his being and it's a story familiar to Husker fans.

"We played Kansas State at home and my dad took me to the game. We sat in the West Stadium and the house was freaking rocking," Caputo said. "I remember feeling that vibration in my chest, and I don't remember everything about the game, but I remember that feeling. It was a night game, and I thought it was the coolest feeling in the world and I was hooked as a Husker kid from then on."

Watching guys like Dominic Raiola (Huskers center 1998–2000) and Toniu Fonoti (Huskers guard 1999–2001), as well as his father Tony Caputo who played offensive line at Kearney State, shaped Caputo's love not only for Nebraska but his desire to be in the trenches, to be an offensive lineman.

"I just thought all those guys were awesome and I was the weird kid who thought it was cool to be an offensive lineman," Caputo said. "I was even a Husker football player for Halloween one year."

It wasn't always a given that Caputo would play for Nebraska, however. Caputo attended Millard North High School in Omaha where he was indoctrinated into a powerhouse program at the time. The Mustangs won a state championship his freshman year and he became a standout two-way player, helping lead Millard North back to the championship in the following three years, winning another title in 2005.

"The goal in high school was just to win state every year. We had exceptional teams. There were I think eight [guys who] played in college after that, five or six that went Division I and a couple still playing," Caputo said of his high school teams.

"I was focused on Millard North, no doubt, and at that point it wasn't just Nebraska. I just wanted to play and I wasn't quite sure where that was going to lead to and it wasn't until I started the recruiting process that those feelings revamped in my mind."

After earning Class A All-State honors by both the *Lincoln Journal Star* and the *Omaha World-Herald*, Caputo was recruited and offered spots by several Division II schools including Central Missouri, Nebraska-Kearney, and Northwest Missouri State, but none of those offers or opportunities matched the level at which he knew he could play. His size was an issue and he knew it, and the coaches at the Division I level knew it, but that didn't deter Caputo. Mentally he always played above his stature and he took his opportunity after a recruiting trip to Nebraska to prove it to himself.

Imagine the scene in *Fight Club*, where the initiates are standing on the porch in front of the house. Someone from inside comes out and tells them go home, you aren't big enough, strong enough, you would never be part of the mission. As Caputo tells the story, that's the picture that plays in your mind.

He speaks with more passion now.

"I went to Nebraska and I had been in contact with Jon Osterhout, the offensive [graduate assistant] at the time, and he's a really good guy,"

Caputo said. "But when I met him, we didn't know each other and I was a little scrub walk-on dude, 6' tall, 260 pounds maybe on a good day, and he's looking at me going, 'What the hell is this kid doing at Nebraska? This dude is going to wash out so quick.'"

At the time Nebraska was returning a beefy offensive line including senior Brett Byford (6'3", 300 pounds) who was a preseason candidate for the Rimington Award, junior Matt Slauson (6'5", 335 pounds), juniors Mike Huff and Andy Christensen (6'4" and 6'3", 300 pounds) and towering juniors Lydon Murtha (6'7", 305 pounds) and Carl Nicks (6'5", 330 pounds).

As Caputo tells the story, you can sense he's fired up and back in that moment. "So my preferred walk-on visit with [Osterhout] was I showed up to the West Stadium and he's wearing these big ol' ostrich boots and he's like, 'Mike Caputo? Nice to meet you, follow me. That's the training table, that's the academic center,' and so on. We walk on the field, and he's basically telling me in so many words that it might not be a good idea to walk on. He said they were looking at me as a walk-on but it's a tough road. Basically, we're looking at you, but we're *kind of* looking at you. It was maybe a 15-minute deal. We didn't even go to the weight room and he walked us right out the front door. Even my dad was thinking, 'I'm not sure they want you to come.'"

It would have been easy, and somewhat understandable, for Caputo to go play in Division II and have a great career helping a Midwestern team, be it Kearney or Central Missouri or whichever, to the playoffs or a championship like in high school. However, he wasn't cut from that cloth. His mind dreamt bigger, and he wanted more.

"And that crazy experience actually made me want to come," Caputo said "I've always been the kind of guy that wants to prove people wrong, and when they tell me I can't, I'll show you I will. It would have always bothered me if I would have settled."

So the decision was made and there he was on campus that first day, looking around the locker room for his name. The equipment manager

Mike Caputo (58) locks up with an Iowa State defender in 2009. Caputo went from walk-on to starter in his Huskers career. *(Courtesy of Mike Caputo)*

had to break the news that he wasn't in that locker room. He and six other walk-ons weren't even in the auxiliary locker room, but relegated to a referee locker room. All Caputo wanted to do from that point on was move up and get better.

Enter Ndamukong Suh. During his redshirt year Caputo was fighting for time on the scout team, and his daily task was to line up nose-to-nose with Suh, which Caputo considers the best thing that could have happened to him.

"Going against him every day grew me up from being a high school guy to really growing and understanding," Caputo said. "He stopped liking going against me because I was like the scout team All-American dude that was trying to prove himself every day, and he was already proven and trying to get through practice. And there I was getting after it every play. It really grew me up and taught me the game."

Linebacker and fellow walk-on Austin Williams saw that fire in Caputo as well. "He brought it every play of every game, even in a bowl practice when some guys would not go as hard. You had better be ready to go with Mike coming at you," Williams said.

Jacob Hickman took Caputo under his wing, teaching him the Xs and Os and intricacies of a pro-style offense, though Caputo had only run option in high school. Although Caputo says he fought "every damn day," that year was hard for him. The freshmen were regimented from 5:00 AM to 9:00 PM with meetings, class, practice, and mandatory study time, and he relied on his support system heavily that year.

During the interview, a knock comes at the door of Caputo's office at Markel. It's his sales manager. When he leaves, something changes and Caputo starts talking about the business, almost with the same passion he talks about football. He talks about the dealership's mission of integrity-based selling and quotes a Gallup poll—about 91 percent of car buyers say they would rather go to the dentist. His father has trained him heavily in haggle-free selling and the merits of the after-purchase experience, which he is teaching to his sales group. Maybe the passion is because this is the family business and he's grown up in it all his life, but maybe it's rooted more in the support he's always gotten from his family, and now he wants to honor that in his post-football life.

"Dad was always very supportive," Caputo said. "His standards for me were always high and he was always looking for the positive. He said people know when they screw up, especially little kids. He knew that I knew when I screwed up, so he pointed out the positive.

"As a parent you don't have to beat your kids down. And I feel like my dad did a really good job of instilling that in me because football coaches are the complete opposite. They will beat you over the head until you get it right."

Caputo's father was at almost every single game going back to pee-wee football. He was a regular at Nebraska practices and perhaps the most important role he played was in Mike's pre-game ritual.

"I would listen to a message from my dad. Before every game in high school or college, he would leave me a voicemail with life lessons—play passionate, play aggressive things like that," Caputo said. "But if I didn't have that message I would have freaked out because I had to have the routine."

His mother also kept him and the rest of the family sane. Caputo refers to her as the glue and he admitted to her during his freshman year that he didn't know he could get so much done in one day.

"When something consumes you as much as a Division I college sport does, sometimes you don't want to talk about it. So my mom was great about that. She never brought up football unless I did. She was the head of the support system, not only for me, but for our whole family. The unbelievable glue that held us all together," Caputo said. "And the rest of us were freaking crazy."

Things fell into place. After Caputo's redshirt freshman year, the Huskers graduated many off the line, naturally allowing him to move up. Caputo moved into a leadership role as he moved up the depth chart and into the starting center position. He never felt like an underdog regarding his size or role. As his responsibilities increased, he realized that he had to take a leadership stance, guiding an offensive line that, throughout his career sometimes was a MASH unit. It was something he embraced, even looked forward to, and the lessons his father taught him showed through.

"It's like anything else in life. To lead is to serve. A leader is only a true leader if people choose to follow, and that takes trust and respect and first and foremost doing your job," Caputo said.

So finally he was in the starting lineup, quite literally the center of attention, flanked on all sides by bigger, taller guys, but Caputo played to his mentality, not his stature.

"I never felt like an underdog regarding my size. Nobody ever believes me that it wasn't a disadvantage, especially at center. Raiola was my height, I've met the guy, I stand eye to eye with him. Casey

Wiegmann played for 16 years and was my height. Mike Webster for the Steelers was a little guy. Throughout every generation you can find great centers that were smaller. If you're quick and tough and smart, you can be a damn good center.

"I never felt like I was that much smaller than everyone, but in truth I was that much smaller than everyone. All the other O-linemen were at least 6'4" and 300 pounds," Caputo said. "I didn't see myself that way. When your coaches say its 90 percent mental, it truly is, especially if you believe it. Tiger Woods is the best golfer in the world when his mind is right. It's between your ears, it's what you believe [that] becomes reality. I believed I was better than they guy across from me, so I was just going to make that happen."

Not only did he look the part, as he still does, but he was mentally the bigger, tougher man. He was outworked, outhustled, and never quit. Teammates noticed, and followed his lead.

Joey Felici, also a walk-on, took inspiration when Caputo came to speak to potential walk-ons while Felici was still in high school. Caputo preached that opportunity came if you worked hard, but to always ask "What if?" And when Felici got to see Caputo in action, he too was impressed.

"Mike was a freakishly strong guy and his motor never stopped. He would follow the play downfield, always running, even in the end zone with the running backs on long runs."

Ron Brown, a longtime assistant, recognized Caputo in a speech about the walk-ons in 2010.

"The walk-ons we coach today are special men," Brown said, making a special point to acknowledge Caputo.

"Every team we play has said, 'Who is that center? That guy is a heck of a player,' and he is," Brown said. "Well, he's a walk-on player and he's earned a scholarship. He packs a lot on that short body, but I'm telling you, that guy's quick, he's fast, and he's smart, and that's what it's all about."

Mike Caputo was a captain for the Kansas game in 2010 along with Tyler Legate and Eric Martin. The game was the last meeting with Kansas as conference foes, and NU won 20–3. *(Courtesy of Mike Caputo)*

Through his career, Caputo rose from walk-on to All-Conference honors and was named a finalist for several awards, winning the Tom Novak award in 2011. His senior year he lined up against six noseguards that got drafted and anchored a line that led Nebraska to nearly 3,000 rushing yards and a 9–4 record in its first Big Ten season.

If only the NFL had seen Caputo for the giant he actually was. After a couple workouts in Minnesota, and a season with the UFL's Omaha Nighthawks, Caputo had to face the reality that his football playing days were likely over. As with most athletes, it wasn't an easy conclusion.

"My transition was difficult for me. You learn all this info, you study all the time, dedicate yourself to working on footwork and technique and you're so focused on a career. This is my purpose in life, these are my dreams and you're living it," Caputo said. "And when it's over, you're kind of in this what-now phase. 'What else am I that passionate about?' You're working with this diverse group of people. There is this big mish-mash of guys that become your best friends and you go through hell together and you have such a purpose together and then one day it's just over. There is all this information I have now, that I don't need. I can't put on a job application that I know a 72 protection."

So Caputo has come home, back to the family business, learning golf because his father said he had to learn golf to be in the business world. He's hoping to get a football camp up and running to train youngsters and future Caputos and feed his football fix. It's clear that these things will always be a part of Mike: family, football, and now business. And he will always adapt, always carry a passion, and always look the part.

—*Brian Brashaw*

CHAPTER 23

JARED CRICK

Defensive Tackle, 2007–11

Every other player had already departed the locker room late that Saturday night, many of them headed out to celebrate Nebraska's stunning 34–27 come-from-behind victory over Ohio State on October 8, 2011, in Memorial Stadium.

Only Jared Crick remained. He'd stayed to meet with an orthopedist and team trainers after he suffered a pectoral injury in Nebraska's Big Ten Conference home debut against the Buckeyes.

Crick was in the shower when he learned the devastating news. He'd suffered a complete tear of his pectoral muscle and would miss the remainder of his senior season with the Cornhuskers.

Feeling somber, frustrated, and uncertain, Crick was thankful for immediate support. He remembers, and won't soon forget, the man who was there to both console and encourage him at that moment—Bo Pelini.

Sure, the Nebraska head coach could've been out celebrating or doing interviews—or anything, really, besides sticking behind until the wee hours of Sunday morning to stay by Crick's side.

"He came down and he talked to me for a good 15 minutes, told me how everything would be all right, the pec would heal, and [that I was] going to be a good football player in the NFL," Crick said. "He just pretty much told me to keep my head up and he loved coaching me and that I'll still be a part of the team. Just everything you want to hear after finding out you'll be done for your senior year.

"He could've been elsewhere, living it up, but instead he comes back down in the locker room to tell me the things I needed to hear that night."

Crick tried to put on a tough face for his coach.

"But deep down, I was heartbroken," he said. "I had come back my senior year to do a lot of good things, help my team win, get as far as possible."

That season didn't transpire as Crick had planned.

"I'll admit it," he said. "My year was pretty terrible."

What Pelini didn't know, and Crick surmises none of the coaches did, either—or anybody, for that matter—is that Crick had already been playing hurt.

A few weeks earlier, in a home game against Fresno State, Crick reached out with his left arm in an attempt to sack sophomore quarterback Derek Carr (who would be a second-round NFL Draft pick in 2014 by the Oakland Raiders). Crick barely got a piece of Carr's jersey.

"My momentum was driving me past him, he stepped up in the pocket, but my hand still had a piece of his jersey," Crick said. "I'm sitting there just really trying to rip him down with one arm, and he pulls up and gets away."

At that moment, Crick felt a burn in his pectoral muscle. He didn't think much of it. Probably just the wear and tear of another grinding game. He figured the pain would go away after a few days, but even when it didn't, Crick didn't feel it was so bad he couldn't continue playing.

So he did. And he kept the injury to himself.

"I wasn't going to tell anybody," Crick said. "This was my senior year. I didn't want to hurt my draft status. I'm not going to tell anybody I'm hurt."

Crick began to play through the injury but suffered a concussion the next game against Washington—a blessing, in a way, he thought, because it would give him time to rest the other injury that nobody else yet knew was bothering him. He sat out a game at Wyoming and returned for Nebraska's first Big Ten Conference game, at Wisconsin, but he didn't feel the same strength and mobility.

"People were, 'Oh, he's not the player he used to be, what's wrong with him, he's not producing.' I didn't tell anybody because I didn't want anybody gunning for me or anything like that."

Then the Ohio State game happened.

"Something happened. I made a tackle, and it just gave out. The entire tendon came off the bone," Crick said. "I think it's one of those things where it just gave out, and that was that. That was kind of a bummer. I was fortunate enough to have it 100 percent healed after a couple of months. It was a rough deal, but it's just one of those things where you come back for your senior year and you don't want to disappoint, but at the same time, you don't want to ruin your draft status."

Crick had never experienced an injury of that magnitude. He didn't realize the significance of the injury and thought that, over time, he would be okay. But he wasn't, and in hindsight he knows he should've handled the situation differently.

"I honestly don't think they knew I was hiding it," Crick, a fourth-round pick in the 2012 NFL Draft by the Houston Texans, said. "I haven't really told many people about it. Not many people ask about it anymore now that I'm in the league and I'm healed. Nobody's like, 'Man, what happened your senior year?'

"I thought I could gut it out. If I knew, obviously, it was going downhill, I would've told somebody and I would've had it checked out a little better."

Part of Crick's stubbornness stemmed from a mindset he developed during his recruiting process, and one that took root his junior season, when Crick and the Cornhuskers were preparing for life without All-American and Heisman Trophy finalist Ndamukong Suh.

Folks doubted Crick, and that fueled him. That, he said, was key to his progress in his five seasons at Nebraska.

"You can obviously say hard work and all of that, but really, for me, the biggest thing was all my doubters," Crick said. "Before I even got to Nebraska, I had a ton of people—classmates of mine, just telling me how there's no reason I should be going to Nebraska...stuff like that.

"I was fired up by that and I wanted to prove everybody wrong."

Being from Cozad, Nebraska, Crick naturally grew up wanting to play for the Cornhuskers. The first NCAA Division I school to realize Crick's potential and offer him a scholarship, though, was Kansas. Soon after, an offer came from Kansas State. Then Iowa State. Some Big 12 Conference South Division schools began talking to him, too.

"If Kansas wouldn't have called, maybe not a whole lot of other people would've called," Crick said. "Seems like if one team sees another team is going after somebody, obviously they're going to check in to see why they're looking at that kid. Not a lot of recruiters come out to Cozad, America, to check out a kid. I figured they kind of leap-frogged off each other."

Finally, the summer before Crick's senior season, Nebraska, then coached by Bill Callahan, made an offer. But Crick didn't jump immediately at his dream school. He was extremely loyal to Kansas, the school that first noticed him and was relentlessly pursuing him. Plus, the Jayhawks were turning their program around under Mark Mangino.

"I waited it out for a while," Crick said. "At the end of the day, I could go to Kansas, maybe do my part to help the team turn around, or I could go to Nebraska and have a better chance of winning a national championship and playing for the home state."

Crick joined Nebraska in 2007 and redshirted. Among the players he battled every day as a scout team player was future Pro Bowl offensive tackle Carl Nicks. In fact, the first time Crick donned pads in practice, Nicks stood across the line from him.

"I had to go against him every single rep," Crick said. "The power that he had, the agility that he had for a guy as big as he was, that was pretty surreal for me. That was a moment I knew I'd have to pick up my game if I wanted to play at that level. He was one of the best offensive linemen in his time, even at the NFL level. Going against him every single day and having him work me out, that was a lot of fun. I think it helped further my career."

Team-wise, though, the 2007 season was a forgettable experience. The 5–7 fallout ended with a 65–51 loss at Colorado and the firing of Callahan. Kansas, meanwhile—the team Crick could've joined—defeated the Cornhuskers 76–39 and went on to win the Orange Bowl.

"I figured I would stay the course, but it was tough," Crick said. "Being my first year in college football, all I knew was a terrible season. It was just rough all around. Guys were out of it. They hated football. They hated life. They wanted nothing to do with it. After the season, after Callahan was fired, we weren't going to a bowl game, and guys were relieved. They were ecstatic, I guess, not to be playing football anymore. Guys didn't want to go to a bowl game. I wasn't playing, so I really didn't know how to feel.

"It was really tough, but I figured I would wait it out, see who the next coach would be, and after they said it was going to be coach Bo Pelini, I guess guys were excited. We knew the fan base really wanted him, and he was at LSU when they won the title. He had championship experience coming in for us."

Pelini and his brother, Carl, who served as defensive coordinator, helped develop Suh, one of the most decorated Blackshirt players in Cornhuskers history. To say Suh was a gifted athlete would be an understatement. He played soccer as a child, after all. But what separated Suh from others, in Crick's eyes, wasn't just his natural ability, but his preparation.

"It really paid off for him," Crick said. "He spent extra time in the film room. I can remember countless times, I was a sophomore and he was a senior. We were watching film, we'd be watching together, and I'd be ready to leave, and he'd sit there and ask me to watch one more game with him. That one game would turn into about three games and countless numbers of cut-ups. He kind of showed me the ropes of how to prepare.

"As a sophomore, I went in and I knew the ropes a little bit, but as far as the preparation, the film watching went, I was just ready to play games. I didn't really care about who I'd be going against or anything like that. I just kind of wanted to hurry up and play the game. He taught me how to watch my opponent, the tendencies they use and different kinds

Jared Crick (middle) with ESPN reporter Niki Noto and Jonathan Drubner in 2011 at Memorial Stadium. *(Eric Beaudry/Beaudry Filmworks)*

of things they would attack us with. That really set us on the same page, I think, just us in there all those nights, about what they're going to do, if they came at Suh a certain way, what responsibility would I have then, or if I did that responsibility, what would Suh's new responsibility be? It worked for us. We were on the same page always, and we had a pretty good duo going together."

Crick also marveled at Suh's pure strength. No matter if Suh was taking on a double team or engaging in a one-on-one battle, he never lost ground.

"It was kind of fun watching Ricky Henry, who's a pretty tough kid in his own right, go against Suh every day and watch the battles they had," Crick said. "As tough as Ricky is, he wasn't moving Suh too far. Those guys made each other better."

Of course, when Suh left after the 2009 season, Crick's doubters surfaced again. Surely he couldn't duplicate his impressive sophomore season, now that teams didn't have to worry about the guy playing next to him. Suh made Crick. No way would Crick be the same player without him.

"And at the end of my junior year, I had better stats than I did my sophomore year," Crick said. "And after my junior year, it was, 'Oh, he's not going to be good enough to be in the Big Ten, the Big Ten needs some big defensive tackles.' Mind you, we were rolling at about 280 at defensive tackle. In the Big 12, we were more positioned to be agile than to just sit there and fill the gaps, stuff like that. It was kind of a knock, 'Oh, he's too small to be in the Big Ten.'"

He proved his critics wrong, and he had some fun along the way.

Crick recalls two-a-day practices his sophomore year when the defensive line crew of Suh, Barry Turner, Pierre Allen, Terrence Moore, Baker Steinkuhler, and Crick grew tired of wearing required knee braces—or, as Crick described them, "big chunks of metal" that cut off blood flow.

"You can barely move your legs. They're really just meat-grinders. Your legs go through a terrible workout, just running with them on."

So the group concocted a plan one day that they simply wouldn't wear them. Nobody would notice.

"We go out, we stretch and stuff," Crick said. "After the beginning part of practice, coach Carl [Pelini] runs up to us, screaming at us, asking us where our knee braces are. We thought there were bigger things on the agenda other than to worry about knee braces.

"He sits there and screams at us and yells at us and tells us to go back inside and put them on. It's kind of nice for us. We get out of practice for 10, 15 minutes, go to the locker room, switch out.

"So we all went up and figure it would be business as usual when we got back, and we'd be ready to practice. He just let us have it for another

10 minutes. All the other individual groups are doing their individual drills, while we're over in the corner getting screamed at like a bunch of little kids because we didn't have our knee braces."

The defensive linemen never again practiced without donning their knee braces.

Crick also learned, courtesy of another scolding from Carl Pelini, to get out of a referee's way when standing on the sideline.

In Crick's defense, the sideline quarters at Boone Pickens Stadium in Stillwater, Oklahoma, are extremely cramped. Players are nestled against the stands. That's part of the reason Crick and Moore drew a 15-yard penalty in a 2010 game at Oklahoma State even though they weren't involved in game action.

They were standing on the sideline when Nebraska quarterback Taylor Martinez, in the midst of a career passing day, completed a long pass down the sideline in front of the Nebraska bench.

"They're coming toward us, and we're probably closer to the field than we are the sideline, and Terrence is a little closer to the field than I am, screaming at something," Crick said. "The ref is backpedaling, the side judge, and he doesn't see Terrence, and obviously Terrence doesn't see him. The ref trips over Terrence. We're sitting there, 'Oh my God, what's going to happen?' because the play is still going on, and the ref's sitting there on the ground, on his back.

"He gets up, looks around to see who it was, and Terrence, he's the closest one, so the ref and Terrence have a little stare-down for a couple of seconds, and Terrence is pleading not to throw the flag and the ref is debating about whether or not he should, and he ends up throwing the flag."

Moore and Crick tried to flee the scene as soon as possible and hide on the bench, acting as if nothing had happened. That's where Carl Pelini found them.

"He sits there and screams at us," Crick said. "I didn't trip the ref but I'm still getting reamed."

Soon after, Bo Pelini followed. Crick and Moore braced themselves for the worst. What they got instead surprised them.

"He just stands there and laughs," Crick said. "It's pretty awesome. It was a pretty tight game, and Coach Bo showed his loose side, especially in a situation where we lost 15 yards."

Crick saw Pelini's loose side, and the next year, in the lowest point of Crick's career, after his pectoral injury, he saw the coach's nurturing side, too.

"I don't know if I would have had the same approach going into rehab," Crick said, "if Coach Bo had not said the things he had said."

—Brian Rosenthal

CHAPTER 24

AMEER ABDULLAH

Running Back, 2011–14

There is a list of well-known things for which Nebraskans can thank the state of Alabama. Add Homewood, Alabama's Ameer Abdullah and his prolific career as a Cornhusker to that list, which also includes such star players as fullback Andra Franklin from Anniston, Alabama, defensive end Dwayne 'Deebo' Harris from Bessemer, Alabama, and the rock group Lynyrd Skynyrd ("Sweet Home Alabama" and "Free Bird").

Lesser known things for which Nebraskans can give thanks to the Yellowhammer State are Alabama coach Nick Saban, who told Abdullah he wasn't a college running back; the proliferation of MoonPies (Alabama holds the largest MoonPie Festival in the country on New Year's Eve in Mobile, Alabama); and Otis Leverette.

Otis who?

Without Leverette pushing Abdullah as a high school recruit to get the type of scholarship offer he wanted, Abdullah would not have ended up a Cornhusker. In some ways Leverette's guidance was similar to then-Alabama high school coach and soon-to-be Husker coach Jack Pierce guiding Franklin to Nebraska despite University of Alabama coach Paul "Bear" Bryant's objection. Leverette, a former NFL player, continued to push Abdullah not to settle even after the high school player had received some big-time offers, but not at the position he wanted.

"Otis believed in me as a running back when others didn't and most of my offers were as a DB," Abdullah said of the man who would was his trainer in his high school days.

It might seem odd in hindsight that a future All-American running back and one-time Heisman front-runner had a few strikes against him as a high school running back prospect. But the bigger colleges continued to stay away from him as a ball-carrier during the recruiting process, despite how well he was doing at the high school camps put on by colleges to evaluate prospects, usually a launching pad for those players that stand out to get scholarship offers.

Abdullah's height—5'9"—caused many schools to pigeonhole him on defense, despite the success of running backs of all sizes in the college and pro levels over time. In addition to not hitting the unofficial 6'0" mark that many schools use in evaluating running back prospects, Abdullah played at a smaller high school that was not a frequent stop for colleges since Homewood High School was not churning out major college players.

"I was under-recruited and my immediate area didn't have many Division I guys," Abdullah said, "so my school was not a place colleges were used to coming to recruit players."

Even though Homewood is a suburb of Birmingham, sometimes the unofficial science of recruiting gets in routines that are hard to break. Still, Abdullah's own evaluation of himself in 2010 gave a glimpse of what schools could expect if they would give him a shot at running back.

"My best attribute is my vision and my ability to cut on a dime," Abdullah said in 2010. "I try to train myself to cut on a dime."

Leverette's training was based on what skills players need to play at the higher levels of football. He was no stranger to big-time football and knew what a real player looked like because Leverette played four years in the NFL. He was a defensive end with stops in Miami, Washington, San Diego, and San Francisco.

He saw Abdullah play at a family member's game and approached him out of the blue.

"During my sophomore year, Otis came up to me after a game," Abdullah said. "And he said thought I could do some things down the road and began to train me."

Maybe Leverette connected with Abdullah because he was not a star recruit by the biggest schools either yet he ended up in the NFL anyway. He played at UAB in the late 1990s and was a late-round draft selection in 2001. The work ethic of Leverette was the reason for his success as a player and a trainer.

"Otis put me through some of the toughest workouts I have ever had, Nebraska included. We didn't have any restraints like a school—maybe that is why," Abdullah said, laughing.

Having a year with Leverette under his belt, Abdullah would hit the camp circuit in the spring of his junior year. Still an unknown despite a junior year with many yards and honors, he attended a camp that had one of the biggest running back prospects in the country at the time in 6'1" Jeremy Hill. Hill would eventually attend LSU before being a second-round draft choice of the Cincinnati Bengals in the 2014 NFL Draft.

Also, most of the participants at the camp were invited to the event. Abdullah said Leverette had to pull some strings, as well as a registration fee. Abdullah showed the camp organizers he would have been worthy of an invite and maybe they should have offered to pick him up for the camp since he earned MVP honors. He thought his performance might open some doors with some bigger college offers considering how he performed against elite competition.

"I did add a Southern Miss offer but that was it," Abdullah said. That offer joined his East Carolina offer and a host of smaller college scholarships.

Abdullah would attend the Alabama camp in Tuscaloosa and perform quite well among the competition. However, he would need some of the toughness instilled by Leverette, especially after a conversation with probably the top football mind in the state of Alabama.

"I was MVP of the Alabama camp and I got a sit-down with Coach Saban," Abdullah, who played at running back throughout the camp, said. "Then he told me, 'We like your style and we see you as a return specialist in college.'"

Abdullah would use the conversation to his benefit.

"That was tough to take, but I was quiet in the car ride with Otis the whole way and I didn't let anybody know," Abdullah said. "I just kept it to myself and kept pushing on.

"Coach Saban didn't know that conversation would drive me, but he helped me build a chip on my shoulder throughout the recruiting process."

That chip would become a boulder with each successive camp that he starred in but unfortunately, the running back offers were few. Abdullah said he started to believe the evaluators' opinions on his college position and he attended Auburn's camp, his dream school, not as a running back.

"At Auburn's camp I played at cornerback," Abdullah said. "I did great and they said they would be in contact shortly. But they weren't."

Abdullah said he was grateful for the attention thus far and was considering taking his best offer to that point before his senior season started, but he still had that voice in his ear.

"Otis said, 'Don't settle,'" Abdullah said.

So Abdullah continued to plug away and again showed it on the field in conference games and high school all-star games as well. In the Alabama-Mississippi all-star game, he gained 188 yards rushing with five tackles in one half of play.

His high school heroics earned him the nickname "Touchdown Bundy" from his brother, Muhammad, from the fictional Al Bundy in the sitcom *Married with Children*. And in some ways his astronomical high school stats looked more fictional than real. Maybe his 1,800 rushing yards and 24 touchdowns his senior year prompted his first major offer when Texas A&M threw their hat in the ring for his services in college.

However, they offered him a role as a defensive back.

"At first I was really excited by Texas A&M's offer," Abdullah said. "But soon it wore off. And again Otis asked if this is what I really wanted?"

As his high school career ended, Abdullah had plenty of major offers from the likes of Tennessee and USC, but all at defensive back. Abdullah was at Homewood High in January with signing day just weeks away when his fortunes would change. He was sitting in art class and his cell phone rang with an area code he did not recognize. He considered letting it ring.

Thankfully for Nebraska, he did not.

"It was an area code I didn't recognize. I thought it could be a bill collector but all my bills were paid," Abdullah said, laughing. "Still, I almost didn't pick up."

Nebraska assistant coach Tim Beck was on the line and he was offering a scholarship to Abdullah. But Nebraska's offensive coordinator said the magic words.

"Tim Beck said, 'We got your film and we think it's great. We want to offer you a scholarship at running back,'" Abdullah said.

Beck told him a running back, Dontrayevous Robinson, had just left the program and they had a need in the backfield. However, that did not mean the Huskers were depleted, since Pelini had recruited the position well.

Many high school recruits study the depth charts of where they might go to college to play, and understandably so, as opportunity is part of the battle to get on the field. Nebraska was not lacking in studs on campus or guys already committed to the Huskers when Abdullah began to consider the program.

All-conference-caliber back Rex Burkhead was going into his junior year, and it wasn't crazy to think he would be the Huskers' workhorse. On campus and eligible the next season would be highly touted running back Braylon Heard from Ohio, a commit from the previous recruiting class who did not qualify out of high school.

But the biggest name already committed to Nebraska was Aaron Green, a running back out of Texas who could likely have picked his college. However, the presence of all those talented players did not dismay Abdullah.

Not one bit.

"They broke down the depth chart for me but I didn't care," Abdullah said. "I just wanted the opportunity to be a running back in college at a big school."

Abdullah knew Nebraska a was major program but he did not accept the offer on the spot. The young Alabama teenager also knew Nebraska had just moved from the Big 12 to the Big Ten conference, but he wasn't ready for his family's reaction to getting an offer from the Big Red.

"My family was like 'Woo Nebraska!' So I did my own research," Abdullah said. "Ahman Green, Rozier, Lawrence Phillips, Heisman trophies...so I found out it was a big-time school for running backs."

With signing day looming, Abdullah had to move quickly. He scheduled a trip for that weekend, but he soon found out he didn't do enough research on Nebraska weather.

"On my trip to Nebraska I only had a small coat, and I had never seen snow like that," Abdullah said. "But the whole trip itself was great. I was blown away on the visit."

Even though he was chilly, he was impressed with the whole package, including the guys he would try to compete against—such as the reigning running back Burkhead.

"Rex has such a complete game as a hooper," Abdullah said. "Crossing people up, post-game, mid-range, taking alley-oops, 360 dunks. Rex can hoop!"

But it was Burkhead's demeanor that impressed Abdullah most. Abdullah said Burkhead, and the other players, didn't treat him like "a pencil neck geek from Alabama" who was trying to take their playing time but a member of the group instead.

When he got back home to Alabama, he did not waste much time in deciding on his future. In fact, he thought he saw a sign to go play for Nebraska.

"That following Thursday I saw Nebraska plates, and I texted my buddy and said that must be a sign and I canceled my USC visit," Abdullah said. "I called the coaches and said that I would love to be a Cornhusker."

He would arrive in Lincoln in June and start to justify Leverette's and Nebraska's belief in his abilities as a running back. But first he would have to get through what was almost a boot camp.

"That first summer we did more before 9:00 AM than most people do all day," Abdullah said. "It was tough but it got us ready for the season."

That summer a teammate noticed something Abdullah posted on social media. Many people post sayings on social media and then don't walk the walk, but that was not the case with Abdullah.

"I remember on Twitter he posted something about out-working the hardest worker," said Huskers defensive back Joey Felici. "And then he went out and actually did it. It wasn't just talk with Ameer."

Abdullah's strong work ethic might have been hereditary. He is the youngest of nine children, all college graduates, with some having advanced degrees. Abdullah would become a college graduate himself in just three and a half years in December 2014. His parents both worked and the expectation was to earn your keep and stay out of trouble.

Athleticism was also important to the family and he jokingly said he was "the failure" as he ranks himself the fourth best athlete in the Abdullah family. Football, basketball, and track were the sports his older siblings starred in.

Abdullah would need everything in his genes while competing in a crowded field at running back in his first fall camp at NU in 2011. But another teammate said he stood out immediately on the field.

"I remember him being like a water-bug," said Austin Williams, a linebacker. "Right from the beginning his quickness, elusiveness, and lateral movement was just crazy."

Abdullah had his moments to shine in his first fall camp and probably stood out more than the more highly regarded running back recruits at Nebraska. But Abdullah said he did take some lumps from one of the best linebackers in the country.

"In one of my first live practices with Lavonte David, he made an

Good friends Kenny Bell (left) and Ameer Abdullah (8) during a lighthearted moment in the 2014 Spring Game. The teammates were both drafted by the NFL in 2015, Abdullah in the second round and Bell in the fifth round. *(Courtesy of Kenny Bell with permission from NU Sports Information Department)*

example of me," Abdullah said, laughing. "I got the ball in space and I tried to juke him and he threw me backward with my feet up in the air."

The Husker running backs coach Ron Brown knew he had a problem on his hands, although a good one, with so many quality ball-carriers. In an early season running backs meeting, Brown asked for some feedback from the true freshmen backs.

"Coach Brown asked us if anybody wanted to redshirt," Abdullah said. "And nobody raised their hand, so from that point you knew it was on.

"Every day was a battle in practice with those guys. It was about consistency, doing well in pass pro, the little things."

Brown would get the little things out of Abdullah and then some. The Alabama native remembers football and life lessons from Brown.

"Ron Brown was so intense and passionate and taught me so many lessons that will be with me forever," Abdullah said. "Obviously he is a great coach when you look at the running backs he coached at Nebraska, but he taught me to live circumstance-free instead of circumstance-based."

Abdullah was making the most of his circumstances through fall camp; even the recruiting gurus would not have given him good odds on making an impact at NU. As the season-opener neared he had an edge on the other freshman running backs. He shined for his elusiveness and willingness to play on special teams—and not just as a kick returner.

"A thing that stood out to me throughout his career and we really respected is he was trying to play on special teams like us walk-ons," Felici said. "Not just as a return guy, but punt block, coverage, whatever. He did that from day one to his senior year."

Nebraska opened the 2011 season with Tennessee–Chattanooga at home. None of the three freshmen would do much with limited carries versus the Moccasins, but Abdullah would show a spark on special teams. One newspaper writer wondered how he would look if his teammates stayed out of his way on kick returns since blocking kinks still needed to be worked out early in the season.

Husker fans would find out the next week versus Fresno State.

Abdullah would begin to stake his claim as the running back of the future with his play on special teams. He would set the first of his many records versus the Bulldogs with 211 kick-return yards, including a 100-yard touchdown in the fourth quarter that was as timely as it was impressive.

The kick return was badly needed as the underdog Bulldogs were giving the Huskers a tussle in Lincoln. Fresno State actually had a third-quarter lead and was hanging around in the contest. As Abdullah went back to receive the kickoff in the fourth quarter with fellow return man Tim Marlowe, Nebraska only led by two points.

However, the big return almost didn't happen, as Abdullah was experiencing cramps as he stood in the end zone awaiting the boot.

"When we were back there waiting for that kickoff, I could feel a cramp coming on," Abdullah said. "I was thinking to myself, 'Maybe this one better go to Timmy.'"

It didn't and Abdullah responded with a touchdown jaunt, highlighted by a jump-skip move on the kicker that left the Bulldog on the ground without ever touching Abdullah. The nimble return man had nothing but open field ahead, but he could feel the cramp coming on so he had to slow down to keep from completely cramping up. He was tackled at the goal line and tumbled into the end zone for the touchdown and the much-needed breathing room for the Big Red.

Abdullah was a major reason Nebraska did not lose that game. Also, the game was significant because he was the only freshman running back of the three that saw action with the offense behind Burkhead.

The next week versus Washington, Abdullah would add a long return to further cement his place in the special teams starting lineup for the entire season. However, for all freshmen running backs that did not redshirt, carries would be extremely limited. Abdullah was Burkhead's backup for the majority of games and ended up with 42 carries, while Green and Heard had 25 and 24 carries respectively. Abdullah saw action in the bowl game versus South Carolina in the first half with the offense that gave an inkling to what the staff was thinking for the future.

His postseason honors would put an exclamation point on his first year as a Cornhusker and foreshadow a fantastic career. He was named to various All-Big 10 returns team and just about every Big 10 freshman team by the media.

For 2012 Abdullah knew he belonged from his performance the previous year, and he was hoping to see the field more. Displacing Burkhead, maybe the top running back in the Big Ten, was not likely, but Abdullah would train with Leverette like the de facto workhorse at Nebraska. In the offseason, Green transferred to TCU, but a school like Nebraska always has good prospects at running back and Imani Cross enrolled in Lincoln.

In fall camp of 2012, Abdullah solidified his spot behind Burkhead, and the backup would see plenty more action in 2012 than in the previous season. Abdullah had proven his ability and usefulness as a different running back to complement Burkhead.

In the season-opening game with Southern Mississippi, a first-quarter injury to Burkhead meant Abdullah would get the lion's share of the carries versus the Golden Eagles. The sophomore would showcase all-around abilities as his intense training paid off.

He rushed for 81 yards on 15 carries, leading the team. He also caught a touchdown pass from quarterback Taylor Martinez. The all-around player had 161 all-purpose yards, showcasing that he could do both if needed for Nebraska since Burkhead looked to be out a few weeks at a minimum.

Abdullah practiced as hard as he played and he gave the Blackshirts a good workout every week. Felici was roommates with linebacker Trevor Roach, who would be a part-time starter in his career at NU, and he made a confession to Felici.

"Everybody, even Lavonte from time to time, had a tough time tackling him his first few years," Felici said. "My roommate Trevor Roach just said point-blank, 'I can't tackle him.'"

The next week, with Burkhead out, Abdullah would get his first career start at running back. Nebraska was traveling to the West Coast to face a UCLA team with a new head coach but loads of talent. In a back-and-forth contest, UCLA pulled it out 36–30.

While Abdullah played well by rushing for 119 yards on 16 carries, he felt the staff didn't trust him with the play calls like they would have with Burkhead in the game. He went to the staff and told them they could trust him more.

The following week versus Arkansas State, Abdullah rushed for a career-best 167 yards on a career-high 30 carries, showing his durability. He also scored two touchdowns for the Big Red.

Burkhead would return to the lineup the next week. The game was over in the first half as NU clobbered Idaho State 73–7. The following week would be the start of Big Ten play and was also one of the most memorable and important games for young Abdullah to gain the trust of the Husker staff.

With the non-conference season over, the Huskers would open Big Ten play with Wisconsin at home. The previous year Wisconsin had battered Nebraska in its first conference game as a member of the Big Ten. In this game, Wisconsin would be wearing alternative uniforms and Nebraska would be wearing all-red uniforms with black stripes and a black helmet with a red N as usual.

The game did not start well for Nebraska, but Abdullah helped keep the Huskers in striking distance. He sparked the team with an 83-yard kickoff return after NU went down 14–0. The drive stalled and Nebraska settled for a field goal. In the second quarter, NU went down 20–3, but Burkhead and Abdullah rotated on a long touchdown drive on the ground and in the air. Abdullah had 22 yards on three receptions as the Huskers kept the game close. And more importantly, the staff was rotating him with Burkhead.

"The Wisconsin game at home was big for me and our team," Abdullah said. "I helped give the team a spark, and we came back and kept fighting even when it wasn't looking so good. The staff preached keep fighting and we did."

NU had to keep fighting even when it looked bleak. The second half did not start well for the home team. The Badgers tacked on a touchdown early in the third quarter to go up 27–10. But the Cornhuskers battled back by rotating their two running backs.

On a 75-yard touchdown drive to keep NU in the game, Abdullah picked up 34 yards on the ground and three first downs. Also, he added first-down carries on the next two scoring drives in the fourth quarter that both resulted in field goals, giving Nebraska a 30–27 lead and eventually the win in a wild comeback. Abdullah finished the night with 252 all-purpose yards versus Wisconsin; once again showcasing his dual role.

The Huskers traveled to Ohio State with some momentum the next week. The game would be pivotal in Abdullah's career and his workload would increase for the foreseeable future after the game in Columbus, Ohio—but for an unfortunate reason.

Burkhead suffered a recurrence of his injury and his return was set at possibly two months, if at all. Abdullah played well with two rushing touchdowns while amassing 213 all-purpose yards on the night, including a 43-yard punt return to start NU's second scoring drive of the night. However, Ohio State pummeled Nebraska 63–38 as the Husker defense struggled to get stops.

The Huskers offense going forward would feature Abdullah teaming up with quarterback Martinez, the starter since his freshman year in 2010. Martinez made freshmen All-American teams while being Player of the Week in games versus major conference teams (former Big 12 rival Kansas State, plus Wisconsin and Ohio State) based primarily on his running ability. But his arm beat Oklahoma State in 2010 and his completion percentage was good, running quarterback or not.

Martinez's his quiet demeanor would draw criticism throughout his career. But Abdullah focused on his ability to make plays and his competitive nature.

"Taylor was such a competitive guy and he could destroy teams when he got going," Abdullah said. "The game against Michigan State, he was just making play after play and Michigan State couldn't stop him.

"He made a great read on the touchdown pass to win the game when he saw how the DB was playing Jamal [Turner] and he made a throw to the outside."

The Michigan State win was just one of the major comebacks in the roller-coaster season. The defense was having a harder time adjusting to the new league than the offense. But in a pivotal game to get in the driver's seat for the divisional title, Pelini's defense bounced back with a complete game effort versus Michigan in Lincoln and Nebraska won 23–9.

A regular-season-ending win versus Iowa with Burkhead returning in below-freezing temperatures cemented a spot in the Big Ten championship. Unfortunately, heavy underdog Wisconsin started fast and shocked the country with a 70–31 win. Martinez and Abdullah kept it close in the first quarter but the Badgers blew the game open by halftime.

Finally, some experts began to re-think their evaluations with Abdullah making most All-Big Ten teams in some form, even though he was a part-time starter. His strong work ethic would be recognized again with Abdullah being named Lifter of the Year at Nebraska.

Burkhead moving onto the NFL for 2013 would change the pecking order at Nebraska. Heard, who played sparingly in 2012, transferred to Kentucky. But Martinez was coming back and Abdullah would be expected to carry more of the load since he had shown the durability to handle the position in Burkhead's absence. Abdullah went into the off-season with this attitude:

"I knew I was the guy for my junior year," Abdullah said. "That off-season was the hardest I have ever worked."

The 2013 season also saw the arrival of possibly one of the best defensive ends ever to play at Nebraska—and without a doubt one of the most impressive physical specimens ever to play at Memorial Stadium. Randy Gregory was a highly touted junior college transfer, but attention and expectations were scaled back when he had to sit out in 2012 at his junior college with a broken leg.

"I thought the team was set since we were in early August," Abdullah said. "But then Randy walks in the training room at 6'5", 6'6" and a chiseled 260 pounds and looked incredible. Beast."

Ameer Abdullah (8) leads fellow captains Kenny Bell (80), Jake Cotton (68), and Josh Mitchell (5) onto the field during the 2014 season. *(Shelby Tilts of Shelby Suzanne Photography)*

There is a saying in football— looks like Tarzan but plays like Jane. Gregory certainly did not embody that saying.

"Taylor tried a quick out from the shotgun and from a four-point stance Randy picked it off and scored a touchdown. It was just unreal," Abdullah said.

While hopes were high in 2013 with NU's returning skill players, an early season loss put to rest any national championship talk along with a season-ending injury to Martinez. Abdullah would shoulder the load with freshman quarterback Tommy Armstrong now under center.

In the middle of an up-and-down year in 2013, Abdullah would make a big play that set up the play of the year for the Huskers. And, more importantly, the play would keep them in the Big Ten conference race versus Northwestern.

The previous week Nebraska had lost to Minnesota as double-digit favorites. Abdullah played well with 165 yards on only 19 carries, but the Golden Gophers rallied for the win. That effort culminated in his sixth 100-yard rushing game in a season that was only seven games old. While Abdullah was off to great start in his first full year as a starter, another conference loss would be damning.

Northwestern jumped on Nebraska quickly, going up 21–7 in the second quarter in Lincoln. But Pelini's defense responded and shut down the Wildcats as the offense chipped away behind Abdullah and a quarterback combo of Armstrong and Ron Kellogg III.

The game was tied late but an Armstrong interception in Nebraska territory gave Northwestern great field position. However, they were only able to kick a field goal. NU took over with a minute remaining. The Huskers faced a fourth-and-15 at their own 25-yard line. Kellogg checked down to Abdullah who made multiple Wildcats miss to get the first down.

"Ameer Abdullah came up big for me," Kellogg said after the game acknowledging the big play when he and receiver Jordan Westerkamp would get the vast majority of accolades for the win. (Kellogg would throw a Hail Mary touchdown to Westerkamp to win the game as time expired.)

With a patched-up offense led by Abdullah, the Cornhuskers would stay in the conference race with a key win at Michigan. The running back would be on the receiving end of a pitch to beat Michigan and keep hopes alive for a return to the Big Ten championship, but after the game Abdullah would deflect praise by mentioning a play made by receiver Kenny Bell that kept the drive alive.

However, the regular season would end on a sour note as Nebraska lost to Michigan State and was knocked out of the conference race. Nebraska also lost 38–17 to Iowa at home in the regular season finale. Pelini made waves in the post-game Iowa press conference with his comments.

But Abdullah focused on the big picture with Pelini, who took a chance on him at running back when others would not.

"One time Bo came into a meeting and just sternly told us we need to be doing better in class after looking at some guys' GPAs, because football will be over one day," Abdullah said. "I don't hear coaches at other schools doing that. He was just making us accountable as student-athletes."

The bowl game for 2013 would be a rematch from a year earlier with Georgia in the Gator Bowl. The game would be a low-scoring slugfest in the rain. Abdullah had words of "wisdom" for Armstrong in a runner-up for the play of the year as Nebraska was backed up to its own end zone on a third-and-long.

"In the huddle, I just told Tommy to throw it up there and to trust Quincy [Enunwa] because Quincy is so good with his hands and big body," Abdullah said. "He made a great throw and Quincy made a great play and took it all the way for a touchdown."

The touchdown by Enunwa was key in that bowl game victory. Another wide receiver and longtime teammate at Nebraska also drew rave reviews from Abdullah.

"Kenny is recognized as a great player, but he was still underrated in the Big Ten. Maybe because of his big teeth and big ears," Abdullah said, laughing about the player who would become the all-time receptions leader at NU in 2014. "But Kenny is a quick twitch guy who can do anything on the field—catch, run, block.

"And he might be the best blocking receiver in college, in addition to his 4.3 and his hands."

Abdullah would end the 2013 season with a First Team All-Big 10 selection and an All-American selection (Third Team) as he rushed for mre than 1,600 yards. This would leave him with a tough choice but two good options.

He could return for his senior year and move up the all-time rushing charts at Nebraska while trying to win the Heisman Trophy. He could also try to attain some significant team goals like trying to win the school's first Big Ten conference title, and possibly a national championship.

Or he could go pro and avoid the risk of injury.

Not an easy decision.

Husker fans wanted the best for Abdullah but they also wanted the best for their team. The eloquent statement released by Nebraska from Abdullah gave them relief in January 2014 and bolstered their appreciation for the player and person he was becoming.

In reaching my decision I have had to consider a number of factors such as my family's economic condition, my projected draft position, and my long term success, not just in football, but in life in general. In order to fully understand my decision one must know who I am and where I come from.

I come from a very modest upbringing. As the youngest of my parents' nine children, I have had to fight for just about everything I have gotten. Despite these apparent obstacles, my parents were able to instill in their children the importance of family, education, and taking advantage of life's many opportunities.

In holding true to these values, all of my siblings have completed their college education with many of them even going on to obtain advanced degrees. Despite my family's tradition of completing its college education, I find myself in a very unique situation of having to decide between pursuing my dream of playing in the National Football League and breaking from my family's tradition of completing our education.

While it may be true that none of my siblings were presented with the possibility of playing professional sports, it is equally true that the average NFL career, because of the violent nature of the sport, is less than five years. In analyzing these truths, I have come to realize that life is bigger than football, and that my chances of long-term success in life will be greatly enhanced by completing my college education.

Although I have always wanted to play in the NFL, at this time I would like to formally announce my intentions of returning to Nebraska for my senior season.

If playing in the NFL is truly in God's plans for me, then God will again present this opportunity to me after I complete my college education.

Or as Abdullah was known to say in the months after his decision with his large family of college graduates, "An Abdullah never goes anywhere without a diploma."

With Abdullah back in 2014, Nebraska was a legitimate contender for championships by having one of the best running backs in not only the Big Ten, but also the country. However, the Cornhuskers would be breaking in a first-time starter in Armstrong, who had his moments in 2013 while filling in for Martinez but also some hiccups, including the Michigan State game.

The preseason focus was a non-conference game with long-time nemesis Miami, but Nebraska was almost tripped up before the Hurricanes blew into Lincoln. As pumped up as the Miami game was, there was little fanfare for the McNeese State game two weeks prior. This was understandable with Nebraska being a three-score favorite. NU fans were hoping to see some backups and have the Huskers play an injury-free game as well.

McNeese State did not get the memo.

NU started out fine with a 14–7 lead and looked to take control of the game in the second quarter. Nebraska was looking to put some breathing room between themselves and McNeese State, driving deep into Cowboys territory. On the 6-yard line, Armstrong dropped back and threw an ill-advised pass that was picked off. It was returned for a touchdown and a possible 21–7 lead, or at least 17–7, became 14–14.

Maybe NU tightened up and McNeese State got a boost. The

Cowboys were not expecting much anyway. NU led 21–14 at half-time and tacked on a field goal to go up 24–14 in the fourth quarter, so it looked like they would survive a slight scare. But the game almost became a horror show when McNeese State wouldn't go away. With four minutes remaining, the Cowboys tied it up at 24–24.

With less than a minute remaining, Nebraska was driving and looking to get in field-goal position. On a third-and-6 from their own 42, the Huskers were trying to move the sticks and get in position for a field goal to avoid overtime and possibly an embarrassing loss.

Armstrong went back to pass and saw nobody open downfield so he checked down to Abdullah in the flat. The running back made the catch cleanly and headed up field. He broke two tackles to get the first down... and then another...and another. The crowd erupted as he sprinted into the end zone on one of the most improbable and amazing individual efforts ever witnessed at Memorial Stadium.

Abdullah told reporters he was just trying to make a play in the 31–24 win.

"I was just trying to get to the end zone. It's kind of a blur now," Abdullah said after the game. "I didn't realize I broke five tackles, but I'm glad I did...The football gods were definitely on our side today."

When Miami came to town, the university would not call on the gods but some legends of the program with the 1994 national champion Huskers back for their 20-year reunion. The two schools had tangled in bowl games off and on since the 1983 season with Miami usually winning. However, the 1994 Huskers defeated Miami in the Orange Bowl 24–17.

Abdullah sensed right away this was not just another big game in Lincoln during warm-ups for the clash.

"I remember coming on the field for the Miami game and it was just a different and an electric feel," Abdullah said. "I really felt like, 'I frickin play for Nebraska!' It was awesome!"

And an ex-Husker from the 1994 team let Abdullah how important this game was to the NU program, even if he couldn't muster more than a few primal words.

"Brenden Stai grabbed me," Abdullah said, "and he was almost shaking me and he said, 'You better kill them!'"

As usual Miami was stocked with players with All-American potential, and that seemed to be the theme of the pre-game coverage. Abdullah used that to motivate him once the hitting started.

"All the media was talking about Miami and their speed," Abdullah said. "I heard a lot about Denzel Perryman, and he is a great player no doubt, but early on I had a run of only about eight yards but I ate him up. And we just rolled from there."

Abdullah ate Miami up to the tune of 229 yards on the ground in one of the most dominant and complete games played by a Husker running back in a big game, helping Nebraska win 41–31. He did enough with those numbers and intangibles in that game to put himself in the lead group for the Heisman trophy.

Even with all those gaudy numbers a teammate noticed something else unusual about the Homewood High School product throughout his fruitful Husker career.

"Maybe the thing I respected most, even with his great ability, was that he never got big-headed," Williams said. "He just stayed humble and kept working."

In the middle of the hoopla in 2014, Pelini took time to talk about Abdullah's recruitment to Nebraska, which wasn't only because of the running back's ability to shake someone in a phone booth.

"We saw someone we thought was really talented, special, and a great kid," Pelini told ESPN during the 2014 season. "You never know how good they'll be, but we recruited him because we thought he was special."

Abdullah was shaping up to have a special year, and it was looking like it could be historic, adding a Heisman to the Husker program's

Ameer Abdullah (8) would end up second all-time on the Nebraska rushing charts behind College Football Hall of Fame inductee Mike Rozier. *(Shelby Tilts of Shelby Suzanne Photography)*

collection with his big plays and big games. Abdullah was following the path of the previous Nebraska winners.

In 1971, Johnny Rodgers had a punt return for the ages in the Game of the Century versus Oklahoma to boost him the following year to the coveted trophy. Mike Rozier had the memorable short touchdown run versus UCLA that ended up covering about 60 yards as he reversed field in 1983; plus he had 2,000 rushing yards. Take your highlight pick with Eric Crouch in 2001—the 95-yard twisting run versus Mizzou or the pass catch versus Oklahoma to ice Oklahoma.

Abdullah was now getting in that line with the jaw-dropping gallop in the final minute versus McNeese State to win a game that Nebraska might have lost, and now a monster game versus Miami on national TV in which he put the team on his back, cliché or not.

But Heisman campaigns also need health.

A mid-season injury versus Purdue slowed Abdullah, and his playing time and numbers decreased with the physical ailment. A loss two weeks later to Wisconsin was especially damaging for the team and Abdullah's Heisman chances. That defeat knocked the Cornhuskers out of the conference race, and playing for a conference division winner helps a candidacy tremendously.

Wisconsin's Melvin Gordon, another Heisman hopeful, would rush for a mind-boggling 408 yards in a game matching two teams ranked in the top 20 versus the nationally renowned Blackshirts to boot.

Abdullah was nowhere near 100 percent for the rest of the year, but he would still tough it out and close with good games versus Minnesota in a loss and in a comeback win over Iowa. For his career, he would end up second on Nebraska's rushing charts with 4,588 yards. The only running back he did not overtake was College Football Hall of Famer Mike Rozier's 4,780 yards.

The Hawkeye win showcased a young teammate who was in some ways becoming a protégé of Abdullah.

"De'Mornay [Pierson-El] is special player and he will continue to do great things," Abdullah said. "He was so clutch versus Iowa and there will be more of that to come."

The young player had a touchdown on a punt return and almost a second one during the last game of the regular season at Iowa. The youngster also showed he had a good role model even if Abdullah had to jokingly re-direct him.

"De'Mornay came up to me one time and said, 'Teach me your ways,'" Abdullah said, laughing. "And I was like, 'I'm no Jedi, just keep working hard and doing what you are doing.'"

If Pierson-El does that, he may break some of Bell's receiving records at Nebraska. But records only show part of the story about the teammate Abdullah calls "Kenny Bizzle."

"Kenny is a complete leader; he always knew what to say and to be accountable himself," said Abdullah, who was a co-captain with Bell. "And you will hear from him in the NFL."

Abdullah, like Bell, spent the months after the 2014 season ended with a close loss to USC in the Holiday Bowl by preparing to play pro ball in the NFL. For Abdullah the process of getting evaluated by NFL teams might have seemed like college recruiting all over again as other running backs without the same resume or highlights were getting just as much or more ink. Scouts talked about his height at the next level.

Maybe those scouts needed to talk to Leverette who told ESPN.com why he approached a high school sophomore the first time he saw him play football in 2008.

"Ameer might've been 5'3", 5'4" at the time, probably 100 and nothing," Leverette said. "And he catches this punt return and only takes it about five or six yards, but this was like the most electrifying five or six yards I've ever seen."

In April 2015, Abdullah's years of hard work and his decision to return to Nebraska for his senior year paid off when the Detroit Lions selected him in the second round of the NFL draft—and this time, there's no question which position he'll play.

—*Jimmy Sheil*